HUMAN HORIZONS SERIES

How To Succeed in Employment with Specific Learning Difficulties

#Autism Spectrum Conditions
#Dyslexia #Dyspraxia #DCD #ADHD #dyscalculia
#Language and Communication Disorders

A Guide for Employees and Employers

Amanda Kirby

A Condor Book
Souvenir Press (E&A) Ltd

Contents

Success depends upon previous preparation,
and without such preparation there is
sure to be failure.

Confucius

Foreword

Writing this book has only been possible because of the contribution of the many individuals who have told me their experiences of preparing for and being in employment over the last few years. They have helped me to understand some of the challenges, and also to gain an understanding of how they have found ways to be successful. Talking to a range of employers from small enterprises to large corporate organisations has allowed me to see a variety of settings and to recognise a lack of confidence in some employment settings in knowing how to support individuals despite a willingness to do so. I have also tried to listen to advisers, educators, welfare-to-work organisations and employers about what they want to know and what makes a difference in supporting someone with a Specific Learning Difficulty. They have described examples of great practices to me and I want to share these with others to assist both employers and employees to have successful experiences.

Speaking with parents of many adults with hidden impairments also reminds me that having a job is so important, not only for the individual, but for its impact on well-being and relationships.

I have to thank all my long suffering family for putting up with me, especially my son Andrew, who has given me insight and feedback regarding the employment challenges in the UK and has assisted with much of the research for this book.

NB. There are lots and lots of links to websites, blogs, apps and resources in this book. Every effort has been made to test they are all working pre-publication. However, if sites are altered then links may not work, something that is out of our control as I am sure you will understand. Be patient, if you can, and search by the organisation's name if this is the case, and sincere apologies.

Many organisations have been cited in this book. The author cannot be held responsible for the actions of the organisations or the people working in them. They are offered only as a guide and their inclusion in this book does not imply endorsement.

CHAPTER 1

Introduction for employees and employers

The purpose of this book is P provide an understanding of the issues around Specific Learning Difficulties and their relevance to the workplace. This will help potential employees and employers to work effectively together whether the individual has a diagnostic label or not, harnessing their strengths and supporting any difficulties that they may encounter.

Around 10 to 15 per cent of the population have Specific Learning Difficulties, also known by some as developmental disorders, neurodiverse conditions, hidden impairments, or hidden disabilities.

They are described as 'hidden' because they may not be obviously apparent to others. These difficulties can impact on learning skills relating to literacy, numeracy, socialising, concentration, planning and co–ordination. They are life long conditions which may have substantial and long-term adverse effects on the person's ability to carry out normal day-to-day activities.

Some individuals may have reached adulthood without a diagnosis but had difficulties at school that were not fully identified. Individuals with Specific Learning Difficulties have the same range of intelligence and abilities as seen in the general population.

Seeing every individual for their ability, especially those with hidden impairments, makes good business sense.

It provides employers with potentially different views on how to see the world which may enhance the workplace and business. Additionally, knowing how to understand and make reasonable adjustments to meet the employer's duties under the Equality Act (2010) is essential practice in the UK.

This book is designed to help:

- Individuals who have a Specific Learning Difficulty or suspect they may have.
- Employers – under the Equality Act 2010 in the UK, knowing how to support employees is no longer an option but a legal requirement for all employers. There are similar legal requirements in many other countries. Simple strategies consistently put in place can make all the difference to retention and productivity for all staff.
- Support networks – parents, carers, educators and advisers who want to assist in preparing someone for the workplace and/or supporting them if they need assistance once employed.

- Recruitment agencies, supported employment agencies – this information is essential for these agencies as they will be seeking to place and support individuals who have many of the challenges described in this book.
- Occupational Health and Human Resources departments in businesses.
- Occupational therapists, life coaches.
- Careers guidance services.
- Education and welfare-to-work providers – who may be providing training for an individualentering the workplace.

Reading this book

You can approach this book in a number of ways depending on who you are and what you want to gain from the content:

- You can just look up a website or link to a useful app. There are hundreds of links to well tested ideas with many free tools to help.
- You can 'spot' read through a specific chapter on a topic area of interest.
- You can read it from start to finish in chronological order.

It is intended to be an easy-to-use and practical guide, based on sound research, experience and practice.

It has been written mainly to focus on issues specific to the workplace, but does also include information on coping with day-to-day living and managing a new and potentially changing social setting.

Remember, some individuals may be in the workplace and have similar challenges but have no formal diagnosis 'label' but may still be assisted by any of the approaches in this book.

The focus of the chapters

Chapters 1 and 2 give a background to each of the Specific Learning Difficulties, how they present and some examples of reasonable adjustments that can be made.

Chapter 3 to 12 cover all aspects of the route from planning to become employed to starting a job and progressing. These have been written for the potential employee or someone already in employment. However, much of the information and guidance would also assist employers to increase the understanding of the challenges met and strategies for success.

Chapters 13 and 14 have been specifically written with a focus on the employer, but offer information that may also be helpful to all.

The book's aim is to provide information for those with any of the following conditions or for those supporting or working with that person:

- Attention Deficit Hyperactivity Disorder (ADHD) (also including Attention Deficit Disorder (ADD))
- Autism Spectrum Disorder (ASD)/Autism Spectrum Condition (ASC) (also including Asperger's Syndrome)

- Dyscalculia
- Dyslexia
- Dyspraxia (also known as Developmental Co-ordination Disorder(DCD))
- Specific Language Impairments (language and communication difficulties)

NB. Style and content

The style and content of the book have been designed with a range of different readers in mind e.g. those with Autism Spectrum Disorders who may need clarity in some of the guidance and avoidance of metaphors. Some readers may have Dyslexia-type difficulties and may find reading texts harder to do. One reason for providing this text in an e-book format is so that it can be listened to as well as read. It can also be accessed on the computer in a pdf format. Kindle and other e-book readers such as Kobo and Sony have the ability to read the text aloud.

All the ideas in this book are also useful for any individual aiming for employment or for those already in a job and experiencing some challenges, but the ideas have been particularly created for individuals with the range of Specific Learning Difficulties described.

From a potential employee perspective

Moving from school, college or university into a working environment, whether on a work placement or into a full-time job can feel like a steep learning curve for most of us, but for some this can be much more of a challenge. Unsuccessful planning can lead to good beginnings but challenges in sustaining employment, or alternatively, sadly, not even getting as far as the job but stalling at the application or interview stage.

There are many benefits of being in employment. For some people having the opportunity to socialise and work as part of a team can be a real boost to confidence and well-being. For others, dealing with new situations can be stressful and create a feeling of anxiety.

Starting in a new setting usually means meeting new people, learning new tasks and understanding the culture of that setting. Every work environment has their own set of rules to abide by e.g. who makes the tea or when to take breaks and lunch, and it may be necessary to understand all these challenges in order to fit in. Not all of these are always written down, which can make them harder to learn or recognise especially if you have a hidden impairment such as ASD. Learning to understand how colleagues and line managers communicate may be quite hard to begin with.

Having a job and managing home life can also feel like juggling a number of balls and trying to keep them all in the air, and not dropping any. Making sure that home and social life are running OK can be a real challenge and often one or the other can suffer. Managing these choices and planning the week to be able to cope can be difficult for adults with executive functioning difficulties i.e. difficulties with planning, organisation and time management common for those with ADHD.

For some people starting a new job can be exciting but for others it may provoke extreme feelings of anxiety and uncertainty. Fear of whether they can cope with everything and a history of poor experiences in education may mean they lack confidence even though they may be very competent to do the job. Some may feel they have not had enough life experience before going into the workplace and still need some guidance.

First recognising that support may be needed is a good step towards accessing help, but finding out what is available and how to obtain it, can seem daunting. That is one of the reasons for writing this book, in order to provide a central point for some of this information.

To be successful in the workplace requires a 24-hour, 7-day a week view rather than just considering the hours in work, and this can make all the difference in ensuring success can be achieved. This can start with what may seem like simple tasks such as getting clothes ready the night before, and ending the day considering what will be needed to be done the following day which can help to become organised and ultimately save time and reduce feelings of stress.

Seeing the link between home and work is very important. Maybe reflecting on past experiences can assist with this. Sometimes a small problem at home can trigger off a series of events that lead to it impacting in work e.g. failing to pay a bill, leading to rent not being paid, leading to increased anxiety and sleep loss, leading to problems in work through loss of concentration and work rates decreasing, leading to losing your job if it continues for some time, leading to a loss of home as well!

Being well emotionally also helps to function well in any job.

From an employer's perspective

As an employer do you know how many of YOUR employees:

- have ADHD or Autism Spectrum Conditions?
- find reading key information difficult to do accurately?
- have sleep disturbance that is affecting their work because they feel depressed or low?

- are slower at writing reports and often make small errors?
- have organisational difficulties that make it harder to manage their time effectively?
- have patterns of stress (physical and psychological) relating to all aspects of the people and areas in your business?
- know who to speak to if they want to disclose their difficulties confidentially?

Do you feel confident as an employer to know:

- what to do if someone discloses their disability?
- what guidance to give?
- what reasonable adjustments to make?
- what someone's challenges were if they said they had Dyspraxia?
  READ ON ....

In every workplace there will be individuals who have specific difficulties with some aspects of their work that with appropriate support can be effective in their everyday practices. These challenges may not be obvious to you as they are not necessarily easy to detect apart from their impact. Difficulty reading may not be known, just that the person avoids all settings where they may need to read aloud, even turning down a promotion because of it. The person with writing difficulties may feel embarrassed to show others or may be misjudged as being less competent because their handwriting looks untidy. Someone with social difficulties may be thought of as quiet or a loner, and misunderstood rather than seeing why that person has responded in a certain way.

Around 15 per cent of the population have hidden impairments at all ability levels and so will be in every area of business. For the employer, not recognising the challenges and seeing the strengths can result in potentially lost productivity, increased sickness absence and may lead to higher staff turnover. Often the reasonable adjustments that need to be made are neither costly nor time consuming. Small adjustments can include understanding why someone has a challenge in a particular task and so responding appropriately to them.

Understanding and recognising the role as an employer, whatever the size of business, does not only make good commercial sense but is a legal obligation since 2010 (the Equality Act). This Act supersedes the previous Disability Discrimination Act and includes other Acts within it.

This book gives a starting point for knowing more about a range of Specific Learning Difficulties and how to provide a process and procedures in the workplace, however small or large that may be. It gives tips and hints and many links to further free resources.

Not everyone knows they have one of the diagnoses in this book and some people may have made adjustments themselves or avoided the things they find harder in everyday life. Others may read the book and for the first time say 'that's me!' and understand why some things have been so hard at times. Having an explanation for such difficulties and tips to assist can mean, for some, the difference between staying in a job and being successful or sadly gaining and losing many jobs because of the challenges. It may encourage some people to disclose to others and seek support if they need it, or share their success so others can see they can do similar jobs.

A key driver for an employer taking the information in this book on board is a legal imperative one, as well as working towards having best practices.

CHAPTER 2

What are Specific Learning Difficulties?

This chapter outlines each of the conditions and describes the challenges they may present in preparing for and being in employment. In addition it introduces the reader to the terminology associated with these conditions that is sometimes used which can be confusing and bewildering.

What's in a label?

Different terms have been used to describe the overall umbrella of different challenges.

Terms such as:

- Specific Learning Difficulties
- Specific Learning Differences
- Hidden impairments
- Developmental disorders
- Learning disabilities
- Learning difficulties
- Neurodiversity
- Neurodevelopmental disorders

Different professionals use these terms in different ways, often causing some confusion. For example, in America, Learning Disabilities is often used as a term to mean reading difficulties, whereas in the UK it usually refers to people with intellectual disabilities i.e. of lower intellectual ability. Some individuals don't like the terms disorder, impairment or disability and prefer the term condition. Others prefer to describe their challenges and strengths and avoid 'labelling' themselves. Some people prefer to see themselves as neurodiverse and not disabled at all, but just different from others, and it is the world and their environment that is potentially disabling them. This sits in a more 'social model of disability' rather than a 'medical model' where the health or educational professional provides you with a 'label' or diagnosis.

A social or medical model?
Being neurodiverse has its benefits in the way one sees the world. Some may be of the opinion that it is society and their views and approaches which disable you rather than the other way around. This is called a social model of disability. One view may be that if people only understood and recognised the strengths as well as the challenges had by each individual with conditions such as Dyslexia or ADHD and saw them as differences rather than disabilities, this would be a more positive view. This model reflects the Union of Physically Impaired Against Segregation (UPIAS) definition of disability.

(*http://www.open.ac.uk/inclusiveteaching/
pages/understanding-and-awareness/models-
of-disability.php*)

The diagnostic labels professionals use represent a shortcut descriptor for others to understand approximately where the areas of difficulties may be e.g. Dyslexia is usually related to reading and spelling difficulties. However, the downside of using labels may be that some people have a preconceived idea based on their experiences of someone else they have met or read about in the newspapers with a similar diagnosis and then may 'group' everyone with that label as being like that person (for better or for worse).

Understanding the profile of each individual, in the context of their life and their past experiences is essential in understanding who they are.

Consider two people both with Dyslexia. They may both have some reading difficulties, but one may have spelling and writing difficulties while the other may not. One may be very good at art and love to paint, while the other has some co-ordination difficulties and avoids drawing and painting all together. One may have learnt to use a spell checker and be excellent on the computer, while the other is uncertain what would be of help in his office job. One may live alone far from transport to employment, whereas the other may be married and live near to a range of jobs to suit his skills. The outcome for these two individuals may be very different – because they are different.

An individual's perspective

If you are the individual with a hidden impairment:

- How do you describe yourself to others?
- Do you want to be labelled at all?
- Do you talk about the 'condition' and challenges you currently have or have had in the past or prefer not to?
- In an interview situation do you disclose or do you wait till you get the job?
- Do you describe your strengths to others before your challenges?
- Do you see yourself as dyslexic for example, or someone with Dyslexia?
- Do you dislike people referring to you as 'suffering from' the difficulties?

An employer's perspective

Everyone with a hidden impairment is different. The challenges may vary in severity and in presentation, despite the label they may come with, if they decide to disclose.

This means it is important for an employer to ask:

- What are the main challenges for the individual?
- How may this impact on their work?
- What has been helpful in the past e.g. person, environment or task adjustment?
- What makes things harder or more difficult?
- Do you want others to know or not? Is there anything else that could be done that would make a difference to you in the work setting?
- Does the business have some 'champions' or best practice case studies to share with the individual to show what has already been done?

Being diagnosed – or not!

Some individuals will have been given a diagnosis in childhood; others in college or university and some may have recognised some difficulties but not known why they were so. The age one gains a diagnosis may influence the label given. The 'door' the individual passes through will bias this. Some professionals have more training in some hidden impairments than others. Some professionals have limited tools in their tool box, and so may only assess cognitive ability and not co-ordination or vice versa.

For some, gaining a diagnosis may be something they want so they can understand what help or support can be given, for others it allows a way of explaining that their difficulty in the past was for a reason and may have been misunderstood by others. Some adults talk about being ridiculed in school or by parents and are seen as lazy, clumsy, or not bothering. A diagnosis for some can legitimise the way the individual feels or the way they have acted.

The reality is that gaining a diagnosis for an adult can be a long and tortuous process because of a number of challenges in the UK and many other countries.

Gaining a diagnosis – a challenge

- **Service provision** in the UK still varies for all developmental disorders. Some of this sits in educational settings e.g. delivered by an educational psychologist, and some sits in health or psychiatric provision e.g. ASD assessment. Many areas of the UK lack services at all for adults with ADHD and Dyspraxia. It's generally easier to get a diagnosis of Dyslexia than ADHD despite someone potentially having this diagnosis as well or instead. It's a bit like only having one item in one size in stock in a shop. Whatever you ask for you keep getting the same thing offered to you!

- **Knowledge:** It can be a 'lucky dip' if your GP knows where to send you. The GP may know more about one condition and so may send more individuals to a specialist in one field e.g. recognising the signs of ADHD but not Dyspraxia or language impairments.
- **The specific assessments and screening procedures undertaken** to diagnose may be dependent on what 'tools' the professional has been trained to use, access to them and the cost of purchasing these items. Some assessment materials cost over £1000 to purchase so they may not have them, despite being considered to be a 'gold standard'.
- **Time:** Pragmatically assessment quality may vary hugely; some assessments if undertaken comprehensively can take several hours to complete as the professional may first need to gather information from several sources e.g. background history from a parent as well as the individual, and then require an in-depth interview and assessment.
- **What is assessed:** Some assessments are undertaken to provide a specific report for additional equipment or support e.g. Access to Work. This means the assessment is undertaken to provide information for a reason, but may not include information to assist in some aspects e.g. with home life.

- **Age:** The age of the individual and when they were diagnosed may influence what diagnosis or label they have. It is most likely that an adult over 35 years of age would have been given a diagnosis of Dyslexia rather than one of Dyspraxia/DCD or ADHD. This would be due to the fact that these conditions were not so well known 20 years ago. If a diagnosis of DCD was given then this would most likely have been given in the last 10 to15 years, as understanding increased and terminology has changed (and continues to change).

- **Confusion over terminology:** Terms used in the field of Specific Learning Difficulties have changed so much in the last 30 to 40 years and continue to do so. Different diagnostic classification systems are used in different countries and this has an impact on the terms used. One of these is from the World Health Organisation (WHO) and the second comes from the American Psychiatric Association (APA). The latter has brought out a latest version of their directory in 2013 called DSMV. In this version the terminology has changed greatly for some conditions. One example of this is the Autism Spectrum Disorders, and Asperger's Syndrome in particular. In the newest version Asperger's Syndrome has now been removed altogether from the criteria to be used by professionals as a term. The new ASD criteria include Impaired Social Communication or Social Reciprocity, which could mean difficulty making eye contact, a lack of facial expression or no interest in one's peers. Peculiar behaviours or interests technically described as 'restricted, repetitive' could mean a specific interest in trains for example. This has led to huge debate and some confusion, especially if someone already has a diagnosis of Asperger's Syndrome.

Specific Learning Difficulties overlap

Most individuals entering the workplace, if they do have a diagnosis of a Specific Learning Difficulty, will tend to have been given one 'label' or diagnosis and may feel reluctant to tell an employer if in fact they have two or three beause of the way they may be perceived. It is very important to recognise that despite possibly having one diagnosis, condition, or disorder (terms other people use), extensive research evidence shows that **most individuals with one Specific Learning Difficulty usually do not have challenges in just one specific area.**

Your brain does not neatly separate out the different areas of functioning and work in isolation so this is not a surprising reality. It would be like wiring each room in the house on completely separate circuits. For example, when someone writes down a message someone is telling them they are using motor skills, visual skills, literacy skills, focus, planning and attention skills, listening skills, processing skills and not just one area of the brain has been activated to do this task but many, interacting with one another.

In fact there is lots of research evidence from the last 20 years to show that an individual with only one area of isolated difficulty is actually quite unusual. For example, someone with Dyslexia will often have some level of attention and concentration difficulty as well (in around 25–40% of cases) while someone with DCD/Dyspraxia may also have challenges with organisation and attention and may find it harder to socialise with others. Dyscalculia (maths difficulties) often overlaps with Dyslexia and DCD. Individuals with ASD often have some symptoms of ADHD and may have more co-ordination difficulties as well.

The implications of having one condition can also have secondary consequence e.g. not being able to do a task such as taking notes in a meeting, or being able to answer the phone clearly, may increase anxiety. Over time this may lead to feelings of depression. Not being co-ordinated may increase the risk of gaining weight for some as it is harder to be fit and do exercise (even though this may be very helpful), leading to greater risk of heart disease. While mental illness and stress has been recognised as very important in the workplace, the intersection between hidden impairments and mental illness has only recently been more widely reported. The only sign of a hidden impairment for an employer may be the impact on the stress and well-being of that the person, as they may hide it well by avoiding situations that make it more obvious to others. This may take its toll in the long term.

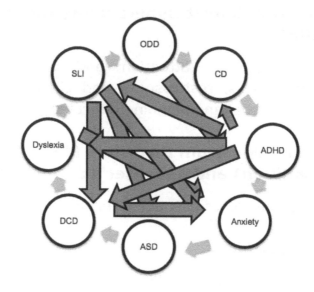

The above diagram shows examples of some of the research showing the overlap between different conditions and the interconnection and overlap between one condition and another.

Unpacking 'Specific Learning Difficulties' (SpLD)

This term Specific Learning Difficulties covers a number of conditions. There is sometimes debate about whether these are learning difficulties or developmental disorders or how they should be grouped together.

Attention Deficit Hyperactivity Disorder (ADHD)

Difficulties with attention and concentration, impulsiveness, restlessness and challenges with organisational and planning difficulties

Autism Spectrum Disorders (ASD)/ASC (condition) and Asperger's Syndrome

Social and communication difficulties

Dyscalculia

Mathematics/number difficulties

Dyslexia

Reading, spelling, recording difficulties

Dyspraxia (also known as Developmental Co-ordination Disorder(DCD))

Co-ordination difficulties in everyday life such as writing, preparing meals, driving a car, playing team sports

Speech, language and communication disorders

Difficulties with understanding and speaking and communicating appropriately and effectively and in context.

Individuals who have any one of the above conditions may also have Tourette's Syndrome, and some may have other conditions such as epilepsy. Other conditions have been noted to be associated as well including Obsessional Compulsive Disorder (OCD), Oppositional Defiant Disorder (ODD) and Conduct Disorder (CD).

Individuals with a Specific Learning Difficulty may also be at a greater risk of symptoms and signs relating to anxiety and depression.

General considerations

- Everyone Is unique, and they are the sum of their past and their present settings and experiences.
- All individuals will vary in severity and pattern of presentation.
- This may also alter over time.
- Presentation of challenges may also be dependent on the demands of the tasks they are being asked to do and the environment they are in e.g. how fast someone wants a task completed; how accurately it needs to be done.
- Hidden impairments usually have an emotional impact for that person and this may alter the way that person can behave e.g. become easily frustrated or angry because others have not understood him or her in the past; someone else not understanding what they have said but not being willing to repeat the information again.
- Past challenges can affect present confidence and self-esteem levels.

- Organisation, planning and time management difficulties can be common with hidden impairments and may not be specific to one.

Considering reasonable adjustments

It is important to consider for anyone the environment that person is being placed in; the skills they have balanced by the challenges of doing a specific task.

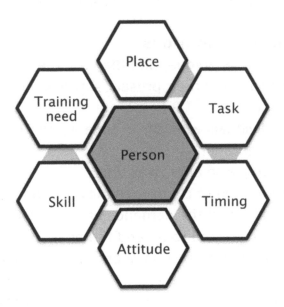

Attention Deficit Hyperactivity Disorder (ADHD)

ADHD affects around 1 to 2 per cent of the population.

Individuals with ADHD may vary in how their symptoms present depending on the level of demands made on them and the characteristics of the environment they are working in e.g. levels of noise.

ADHD can affect both attention and concentration. Although some people are still given the diagnosis of ADD this term is less commonly used today, with ADHD used as the umbrella term.

It is acknowledged that most adults' symptoms of overt 'hyperactivity' become less obvious as they grow older and may rather be feelings of 'inner restlessness'.

Workplace difficulties described by adults with ADHD:

- **Impulsivity**
  This may demonstrate as speaking and acting without thinking, interrupting others, difficulty in waiting turn and lack of awareness of the context in which the person is behaving. Someone may quickly send an email without checking it; send out a parcel without noticing there was an error in the address; miss out a step in a task because they are keen to complete it.
- **Hyperactivity**
  In adults this is less obvious to others and may just be observed by difficulty in sitting still, or being restless and fidgety such as tapping feet or being over-talkative. These behaviours are more obvious in childhood and more commonly seen in men than women.

- **Inattention**
  This can result in the individual being easily
  distracted, having poor concentration, difficulty
  organising themselves and their work without
  practising and automating procedures, starting
  but finding it hard to finish tasks, and/or
  starting a task and missing out steps in the
  instructions. Prioritisation of work may be
  harder to do, seeing what is important from the
  less important.

Workplace example:

Janet is working in an administrative post. She has
different jobs given to her by different team
members, often verbally. She is very keen to do her
job well but sometimes unintentionally forgets some
parts of a task as some people seem to be giving
her several instructions at a time. She recently sent
an email (in work) to her boss, rather than her
friend about a personal matter, which caused some
embarrassment. She finds it difficult to prioritise
without guidance, and can over-focus on one task
and then miss some deadlines for others.

Discussing these issues with her line manager
has resulted in some adjustments being made. One
of these was showing her how to use an electronic
diary and then setting this up with her. Her line
manager spoke to colleagues (with her permission)
about how she has some challenges if only being
told information orally and they now make requests
for work by email as well as giving them verbally.
This has also allowed her to have all instructions

listed in one place and in date order. She and her line manager also sit down together for five to ten minutes a day to prioritise the action list and set deadlines She also has learnt to wait before sending any emails and checking them before sending them out. She has really gained in confidence and she now looks forward to work. She recently suggested some ideas for the business she works in, and they have been implemented.

Strengths noted:

- Ability to focus on areas of high interest
- Good entrepreneurial skills
- Good at project work
- Likes variability
- Sees the 'big picture'
- Can see innovative ways of tackling problems

Reasonable adjustments for employers to make for individuals with ADHD may include:

- Arranging short but regular meetings with the line manager
- Providing written instructions and information, as well as oral ones
- Providing continued monitoring to prioritise the work
- Giving constructive but specific feedback – avoiding being vague
- Showing how to structure tasks and what the completed task should look like

- Setting clear deadlines but understanding that some tasks may take a little longer to achieve especially if this is unfamiliar to the individual
- Subdividing larger projects into smaller units to see specific end points
- Providing clear and structured training
- Demonstrating how to use web-based diary systems to provide reminders etc.
- Showing how to put in proofing and checking mechanisms where appropriate.

Autism Spectrum Disorder (ASD)

ASD is a spectrum of difficulties that affects how an individual communicates with, and relates to, other people. The 'spectrum' element of the disorder means that while all people with ASDs share certain difficulties, their condition will affect them in different ways and to varying degrees.

Individuals may have been given a diagnosis of any of the following under the umbrella term: Autism, Asperger's Syndrome and Pervasive Developmental Disorder Not Otherwise Specified (PDD-NOS).

Autism Spectrum Disorder (ASD) affects about one percent of the population.

Terminology has changed over the last decade, along with an understanding of the condition.

There are diagnostic 'bibles' that have been developed and updated. There is one produced by the World Health Organisation called the International Statistical Classification of Diseases and Related Health Problems (ICD for short) and a second one from the American Psychiatric Association. This latter one has brought out diagnostic criteria in 2013 with the result that the term Asperger's Syndrome and PPD-NOS are no longer present. In the newest version Asperger's Syndrome has now been taken out of the criteria to be used by professionals as a term altogether.

This has led to huge debate and some confusion, especially if someone already has a diagnosis of Asperger's Syndrome. This has resulted in concern for professionals deciding what terms to use and for those already with a diagnosis who are confused about what they have now, and how to tell others.

The new ASD criteria include:

- **Impaired social communication or social reciprocity**, which could mean difficulty making eye contact, a lack of facial expression or no interest in one's peers.
- **Peculiar behaviours or interests** technically described as 'restricted, repetitive', could mean a specific interest in trains for example.

Workplace difficulties described by adults with ASD:

- Difficulty with gaining an understanding as quickly as others of the workplace rules that may not have been discussed e.g. when to take breaks; how to speak to peers and line managers appropriately. This may present to others as appearing rude e.g. making coffee only for themselves and not asking others at the same time.

- Finding it harder to perform well in large group interaction, and having a preference for one-to-one or small group discussions and/or working practices.
- Some sounds, lighting settings, movement of others causing difficulties focusing and engaging.
- Lacking confidence in asking questions or asking for help, or not understanding that help could be given.
- Reluctance to discuss difficulties and articulate where, when and how they impact. This may result in difficulties mounting up until there is a big problem because of being unaware or anxious about dealing with the smaller issues.
- Difficulty with waiting to respond, without being given an explanation for the reason for a delay for example.
- Difficulties with social understanding and communication may result in the individual's behaviour sometimes being misinterpreted by others e.g. arriving late to work but not thinking to tell the line manager the reason why, such as the bus did not come or the car had broken down.
- Appearing very able, yet facing real difficulty in getting to appointments on their own, coping with a change of routine and performing well in interviews.

- Dressing/presenting themselves appropriately for the work setting.
- Staying calm if feeling irritated or frustrated by other people or the environment.
- Coming across to others as confrontational if unsure of what is being asked.
- Experiencing anxiety and having a sensitivity to certain sounds, touch, tastes, smells, light or colour. This may vary greatly from one person to another.
- Being seen as overly honest in a situation.
- Showing feelings to others obviously e.g. yawning when tired, becoming angry.

Workplace example:

Ahmed started working at a retail store helping to mend computers as he had excellent computing skills. However, he had weaker interpersonal skills and was not so good at relating to the customers and listening to them explain their problems. He had been told that he appeared aloof and disinterested by his line manager. When he first started he reported that he found the noise in the open plan setting very loud and it affected his ability to concentrate. He was also irritated by other colleagues walking past his desk which had been placed in the centre of the office thoroughfare.

His line manager arranged an Access to Work assessment and it was agreed that his location would be changed, so that he was facing towards a wall and away from the main flow of traffic. He also started wearing headphones, when specifically working on mending the computers, to reduce the background noise. He has had some specific guidance and training on how to communicate with customers and the line manager minimised his direct contact. His volume of work has increased since these adjustments have been put in place.

He has worked at the store for five years and has never taken a day off sick, is on time every day and completes all tasks with a high level of accuracy and efficiency.

Strengths noted in the workplace:

- Accuracy
- Reliability
- An excellent memory for facts and figures
- Ability to thrive in a structured, well-organised work environment
- Good at detail
- Likes consistency
- Persistent
- Logical
- Systematic
- Good time keeper

Reasonable adjustments for employers to make for individuals with ASD:

- Providing one-to-one rather than group training if needed when first starting in a new job and if/when changes occur to working practices.

- Establishing and maintaining routines so that the individual knows what to expect from day to day and week to week.
- Reviewing the week at a set time and on a certain day.
- Warning as much as possible if work needs to be changed – reinforcing this information e.g. note, email as well as words.
- Discussing if there are specific things that cause an increase in anxiety levels e.g. change in routines, specific noises, lighting etc.
- Explaining changes in routine in advance, where possible, and giving time for the employee to understand them.
- Plan ahead. Discuss, for example, what may happen at a meeting that is planned, who may be there, and what needs to be achieved.
- Avoiding giving too many options or choices.
- Avoiding using abstract or hypothetical language.
- Keeping language simple and avoiding metaphors, and allowing time for understanding and reflection to take place.
- Avoiding joking and making statements not to be taken literally.
- Using gestures to reinforce what you are saying to add to meaning and intonation to your voice.
- Using visual demonstration to support words – pictures, templates, timetables.
- Using verbal cues to reinforce tasks and being prepared to go through a sequence in exactly the same way each time for consistency when training someone. Try to demonstrate all parts

of a task or job so the individual can see where his or her part fits in.

- Avoiding using negative words such as 'not', 'no', 'don't' and explain what needs to be done.

Developmental Co-ordination Disorder (DCD)/Dyspraxia

Developmental Co-ordination Disorder (DCD), also known as Dyspraxia, is a motor co-ordination disorder. The difficulties impact on everyday life skills. DCD/Dyspraxia is distinct from other motor disorders such as cerebral palsy and stroke.

It affects about 2 to 3 per cent of the adult population.

Workplace difficulties described by adults with Dyspraxia

- Skills requiring balance e.g. carrying a tray with glasses.
- Difficulties with small movements (fine motor co-ordination) if needing speed and accuracy e.g. preparing meals using a knife needing accuracy and speed; a dental nurse or dentist doing small and accurate movements in a mouth.
- Difficulties writing at speed and legibly, for example taking notes in a meeting.
- Driving a car – this may take longer to do, and parking and distance estimation may be harder to do.
- Organisation, time management and planning skills including prioritisation.

- Difficulties when dual tasking e.g. doing more than one task at a time, especially if unfamiliar with the task.
- May be slower learning new tasks requiring good co-ordination skills.
- May also affect everyday life skills e.g. preparing a meal, ironing, tying shoe laces which may impact on appearance e.g. shoes undone, shirt hanging out, creased clothing.

Workplace example:

John has recently qualified as a solicitor and is doing his legal articles. He has always had handwriting which appeard to be untidy. He often can't read his notes after meetings which has become a problem as he misread some of his notes after a meeting with a client. Others have also commented on his appearance, that he is not always as tidy and 'professional' as he could be. For example, he sometimes has his shirt tails hanging out and shoelaces undone. On the positive side he has an excellent memory, is very good at recalling information, and is very dedicated to his job. He is always first in the office in the morning and ready to take on any tasks given to him.

His line manager met with him and discussed his concerns over his appearance and what suitable attire for work would be appropriate. John put a 'work uniform' together, including wearing slip-on shoes. His peers also agreed to remind him, if they could, to tuck in his shirt before going into an important meeting.

His line manager arranged an Access to Work assessment (undertaken in the UK); he was shown how to use Speech-to-Text (STT) software and uses this when producing more complex legal reports. He uses Text-To-Speech (TTS) software to listen and check their content (see *Chapter 8*).

Strengths noted:

- Patient, caring and empathic
- Persistent and hard working
- Looks for alternative solutions
- Honest
- Motivated to overcome difficulties
- Ability to think ways around impasses
- Once a skill is learnt it's there for life.

Reasonable adjustments for employers to make for individuals with DCD/Dyspraxia may include:

- Avoiding handwritten tasks
- Using Speech-to-Text software to minimise handwriting or encourage fast typing skills
- Giving adequate time for learning new tasks
- Breaking down tasks into small steps and demonstrating them
- Encouraging accuracy first and then increasing speed once the task has been accomplished
- Adapting or avoiding tasks requiring either very good fine motor skills or balance if they could be a potential risk to the individual

- Providing guidance for organisation and planning where several tasks need to be completed to a deadline
- Demonstrating diary systems and how these can be synchronised with computer and phone and backed up.

Dyslexia

- Dyslexia is a difficulty in acquiring good literacy skills and may include difficulties with reading, writing and spelling.
- It affects about 8 to 10 per cent of the population.
- It is the most common and widely understood of the SpLDs (Specific Learning Difficulties) due largely to its direct impact upon academic success, job prospects and continued gainful employment.

Workplace difficulties described by adults with Dyslexia:

- Taking longer to read documents than colleagues
- Difficulties with structuring a document, and spotting spelling errors may be an issue
- Lack of confidence to ask questions or for help and may appear anxious
- Problems remembering some tasks e.g. attending appointments and bringing the right paperwork to meetings

- Filling in forms, especially if handwritten, can be problematic
- Completing web-based forms that require a time element to complete – as these may 'time out'
- Having weaker organisational skills
- Being reluctant to tell others they have Dyslexia for fear of the consequences.

Workplace example:
John was a police officer and had worked his way up the organisation. He had excellent people skills. Promotion had been duly given to him. Recent changes had increased the need to do more report writing, training of other officers and going to more meetings. He also had to take notes and listen to the meeting. He was worried that if he disclosed to his colleagues that he had Dyslexia they might think less of him and he might be less respected. He was concerned about being able to write down notes accurately and respond to queries. He started becoming increasingly anxious, not sleeping and being irritable with others. His work was affected and he was late with reports. This resulted in his anxiety increasing and him having time off for stress.

Human resources made contact with him to discuss his return to work and the reasons and triggers for being 'off sick' and this revealed some of his concerns regarding his literacy difficulties, and in particular his concern about writing reports under time pressure and without spelling mistakes.

A discussion over return-to-work arrangements took place. He undertook an Access to Work assessment (available in the UK) and was provided with a tablet computer as it was portable and allowed him take notes in meetings. Other reasonable adjustments were made including his development of standardised report templates. These were so useful the templates were then used by other officers across the service. He has been further promoted in the past 12 months and has had no further time off work. He has also offered to speak to other police officers about his experiences.

Strengths noted in the workplace:

- Good at creative ideas and innovative thinking
- Creative in the way the individual makes links and connections
- Good with practical tasks
- Often stronger in the areas where literacy skills are less important such as art, design, architecture and engineering
- Good verbal communication skills.

Reasonable adjustments for employers to make for individuals with Dyslexia:

- Providing training on the use of assistive software and converting notes to pdf format so they can be read aloud, or using Text-to-Speech (TTS) software and spellcheckers

- Giving written instructions and information rather than oral
- Using smartphones for synchronising appointments with the computer so an entry is made only in one place and not lost on pieces of paper or in a paper diary – encourage a backup system
- Using Text-to-Speech (TTS) and synopsis software where there is a lot of reading to be undertaken. This allows the person to hear what has been written and can reinforce reading and spelling skills
- Allowing Speech-to-Text (SST) software to be used to minimise writing and to avoid having to think how to spell particular words
- Allowing all meetings to be recorded and notes given beforehand where possible
- Ensuring supervisors are appropriately trained and understand how it may impact
- Where possible providing automated (including reminders) IT support for functions such as backup and password storage
- Providing a list of industry specific words and acronyms
- Showing how to organise work e.g. use of colour coding, folders; and how to subdivide projects.

Dyscalculia

Dyscalculia affects a person's ability to understand, recall or manipulate numerical information or conceptualise numbers as abstract concepts.

It affects about 3 to 6 per cent of the childhood population. It is not clear how many adults continue to have difficulties.

Some individuals may feel anxious when having to undertake any mathematics related tasks and so may avoid situations where this has to be done, such as paying bills or avoiding specific jobs.

Workplace difficulties described by adults with Dyscalculia:

- Taking longer to read documents and extract the number problems when written in words
- Having difficulties with 'simple' maths tasks, especially if needing to be done at speed
- Having confusion with regard to signs e.g. +, −, or x
- Having difficulties with accurate recording of numbers
- Being confused when dialling telephone numbers
- Difficulties with trying to understand financial information e.g. budgeting, reading a spread sheet
- Difficulties with conceptual understanding of formulas
- Difficulties with time management and being aware of time passing
- Having challenges with estimating distances
- Difficulties when reading and recording long numbers accurately e.g. telephone numbers, bank account numbers

- Getting confused or forgetting pin codes and security numbers.

Workplace example:

Sara has great interpersonal skills and works as a receptionist at a hotel. She has to answer the phone and take down messages as part of her job and this includes recording telephone numbers. She also has to prepare bills when other staff are busy. As a part of her job she has to prepare electronic key cards for the rooms.

She gets along well with the customers but regularly makes mistakes taking down telephone numbers and has wrongly calculated bills on a couple of occasions, and also punched in the wrong codes on room keys. This has resulted in disgruntled customers complaining that they have had to come back to the reception to get another card.

Discussions with her line manager have resulted in her having some specific training on producing bills. A computerised system has recently been put in place which has made it easier for her as well. There are still some challenges despite adjustments being made and she has recently changed roles to help with conferencing and to meet potential clients. She is doing very well in this position and has gained in confidence.

Strengths noted in the workplace:

- Good verbal communication skills
- Problem solver and lateral thinker

- Creative in the way she makes links and connections
- Stronger in the areas of art, music, design, architecture and engineering
- Good at holistic perspectives.

Reasonable adjustments for employers to make for individuals with Dyscalculia:

- When presenting numerical data, reduce data to essential parts and remove unnecessary figures or words i.e. making the message clear and providing clear visual representations such as pie or bar charts
- Going through any number work specific to the job e.g. use of bar codes, pin codes
- Providing facilities for speed dialling of telephone numbers
- Considering alternative passwords and codes not requiring numbers
- Setting up template expense forms and going through them with the individual
- Providing handheld calculators and consider the use of a speaking calculator.

Speech, language and communication impairments (SCLI)

Specific language impairments include:

- Receptive language difficulties – understanding what is being said to the individual

- Expressive language difficulties – articulating and speaking with others
- Semantic and pragmatic language difficulties – understanding the social context of the language – the meaning and intonation
- Verbal Dyspraxia – this is related to the planning of speech movements.

Around 7 to 12 per cent of children in their teens have been cited as having SCLI.

Each person may present with a different pattern of challenges.

Workplace difficulties described by adults with speech, language and communication challenges:

- Taking down telephone numbers or instructions
- Remembering a sequence of instructions
- Taking longer to respond to a request
- Needing to be shown rather than told, otherwise may make mistakes in tasks
- Feeling or appearing anxious/angry if not understanding what is being asked of him/her
- Appearing to others as shy or withdrawn
- Misunderstanding what has been asked of him or her resulting in making an error in work without any intention to do so
- Having difficulty taking turns in meetings
- Preferring to lead a group project rather than be led, as he/she will know what is going on
- Having some difficulties entering or leaving a conversation, especially in a group setting

- Having problems being understood by others – speech may be indistinct to those unfamiliar with them.

Workplace example:

Emma is working in a café in the leisure centre and serves and takes orders. She has difficulty remembering sequences of instructions and has got orders mixed up a few times as she has forgotten what people have said or misunderstood the instructions. Her line manager asked her what she thought would be of help to her. She used a note pad to write orders down, but that was still a problem for her. She decided to leave that job and started a new job with a restaurant that used an automated ordering system and where she was given very specific tasks in the kitchen.

Strengths noted:

- Patient, caring and empathic
- Persistent
- Prepared to look for alternative solutions
- Motivated to overcome difficulties.

Reasonable adjustments for employers to make for individual with SCLI:

- Asking for preferred method of communication
- Providing written information as well as being told instructions

- Giving single instructions instead of several at once
- Checking for understanding when giving instructions, and repeating if required
- Avoiding use of colloquialisms and metaphors or explaining their meaning
- Allowing additional time to respond if processing of information takes longer than expected
- Allowing some additional time for learning new tasks
- Showing how to break down tasks into small steps and demonstrate them
- Providing some guidance for organisation and planning where several tasks need to be completed to a deadline
- Going through the workplace rules and ensuring you are explicit – checking for understanding
- Avoiding making jokes that may be misinterpreted or taken literally in meaning
- Being explicit in what is required and demonstrating where possible.

Reasonable adjustments for individuals with short term memory challenges:

Individuals with Specific Learning Difficulties can have some challenges in common such as with organisation, time management and also remembering instructions.

- Chunk difficult numbers into smaller chunks which are easier to remember – for example a phone number spaced out (020 – 7265 – 1234)

- Use repetition; the more you repeat something the quicker you remember it
- Use to-do lists to see the visual order of actions to be completed
- Always carry a pen and something to write on
- Use a diary system as a reminder for actions and deadlines and set alarms as auditory prompts
- Write important things to remember on Post-it notes and put them in key places where you will see them frequently, for example, the fridge door
- Use associations as a reminder of facts e.g. mnemonics; relating information to a tune; a mind map or specific series of pictures.

CHAPTER 3

Thinking about career choices and matching strengths

This chapter gives some guidance on considering careers and how to think about strengths and experiences that could be used to show transferable skills. In addition what to consider if undertaking voluntary work or work experience. This chapter is aimed at potential employees.

Gaining a permanent job can be very hard for many people today with high levels of competition and the need to be skilled not only in the job but also in the interview and selection processes.

Having some work experience, paid or unpaid, can provide an opportunity to explore different work settings and to help in deciding what type of work and workplace is right and what level of support or adjustments may be required.

For some people thinking about where they could work and the type of job they could do is hard to envision. In some settings work tasters are allowed where you can attend several placements.

In order to even go into a voluntary placement there is a need to decide what strengths, skills or interests are already in existence.

Recognising and selling strengths

The career and individual usually chooses is usually a product of interests, strengths and the qualification or skills achieved, or working towards. However, where there are shortage of jobs then for many of us we have to do a job that is available rather than the 'perfect fit'. This can sometimes give transferable skills that can be used in another setting e.g. such as working as part of a team. The job may not be the ideal one, but all experience can be helpful even if it is only to gain in confidence and have an opportunity for social interaction.

Some people, especially those with Autism Spectrum Disorder (ASD) may have a narrow range of interests and this can make it harder to find a fit with interests and what is available. Selling strengths to employers is essential and it is sometimes the skill of presenting this that allows the employer see the value of the individual e.g. liking working with computers and having a meticulous approach to work can be of great benefit.

When going for work placements or jobs of any sort there is a need to think of positive ways of presenting information, truthfully.
Sometimes people find it hard to recognise their strengths in themselves. This may be the case for someone with ASD who may find it harder to see themselves objectively. For others, it may be because they have heard people only describe their weaknesses all their lives.

Discussing with others who know the individual such as parents, or someone else who knows the person well and cares about them can result in positive phrases to describe them.

Tips to assist for the individual:

- Rehearse responses with someone you know
- Think of examples of what you have achieved over the years during school, college or university
- What hurdles have you overcome despite challenges?
- Ask others to describe what they think are your strengths

- Remember you are not the 'label'. Having a diagnosis or conditon only describes one part of you, and you should not be defined by it. You are not, for example, dyspraxic or dyslexic but rather a person with Dyslexia or Dyspraxia.

Triggers that may help provide examples of strengths:

- Past pleasure in school – a role played, a leader of a team, working as part of a team, being creative
- Current hobbies – what is of interest and why?
- Voluntary work – what is there that is exciting and interesting?
- What was one of the best times for you in your life, what were you doing?
- A place you like to be in e.g. spending time outside
- Being with many or a few people?

Having a list of adjectives can act as a prompt for key words to use as descriptors

- artistic
- a good listener
- creative
- honest
- innovative
- exact
- careful, or meticulous
- musical

- precise
- physically fit
- sporty
- like the outdoors
- good with children or the elderly
- scientific
- have good mechanical skills
- have good IT skills
- come up with new and interesting ideas
- sociable
- logical
- caring
- empathic
- patient
- present yourself well
- hard working
- independent
- good visual skills
- good long-term memory
- able to learn and remember facts.

What are transferable skills?

These are skills that employers look for when they are interviewing, and when applying for a job. It is essential that examples are thought of and developed if uncertain.

Transferable skills are those versatile skills that you can apply and make use of in a number of different roles.

Think about hobbies and interests you have done in the past or do now, or a voluntary position you may have taken e.g. coaching others. Discuss with someone who knows you about activities you do at home e.g. babysitting, cooking or managing a household. Think about what it is about the hobby you do that you like.

e.g. If you like gardening is it because you:

- like being outside?
- like being alone?
- like doing things with your hands?
- like seeing something grow?
- like planning the garden?
- like routine?
- like the physical actions of digging etc.?
- like working with others?

If you have been travelling abroad or in this country, did you do this because you:

- were showing a level of independence?
- liked being able to make decisions on your own?
- liked going to unfamiliar places?
- liked learning a new language?
- liked meeting new people?

Go through the same process for anything you like to do.

Have you helped out at a local football team?

- This could show you have good physical skills, or you are a good team player, you are sociable, you like being outside, you meet new people, you like the social side of playing, or it keeps you fit.

Have you taken a computer apart and mended it?

- This could show you have good mechanical and logical skills, or you are persistent, inquisitive, like working on your own, or are practical.

Have you helped out in a local restaurant in the kitchen or at the table?

- This could show you have catering skills, or are sociable and hard working.

Have you done some voluntary work for a local scout or church group?

- This could show you have good team working skills, you are sociable, like working with children, or it's a good way of meeting new people.

Do you like making cakes or cooking?

- This could show you have creative skills, artistic, methodical, and scientific or like doing things for others.

Defining the ideal job

You will need to have an idea of what kind of jobs you are looking for.

Make a list of criteria for the ideal job based on some of the following questions:

- What have you enjoyed most and talk about enthusiastically?
- Do you prefer working as part of a team or on your own?
- Do you want to work full- or part-time, weekends or nights?
- How many miles do you want to work from where you live?
- Are there good transport links?
- Are you looking for the job to be office-based, outdoors, or a mixture?
- Do you want temporary or permanent work?
- Is shift or night work harder for you because of health or family reasons?
- Do you see this as a stepping stone to something else?
- Are there specific conditions or settings you have to avoid e.g. do you have health or religious reasons for not working in a specific setting?

- Do certain sounds, or noises upset you or make you feel irritable?
- Is communication a difficulty for you and so being in a job that requires this would be harder for you?
- Is your co-ordination poor and could this be a health and safety issue for you in certain jobs?
- Do you have difficulties driving and so may need a job near good public transport links?
- Do you get bored easily and need a job with variety and working in different environments?
- Do you prefer to be in the same environment and like to have a regular and routine type of job?
- Do you prefer a job that requires new ideas or do you prefer something that requires you to research solutions?
- Do you prefer to be self-directed or do you prefer someone to tell you what to do?
- Having a good idea of what would or wouldn't suit you is essential for a job search BUT it is important to be flexible, especially when jobs are hard to come by!

Work experience and voluntary work

If you don't have an idea of what jobs interest you, and you don't have the skills or experience to apply, try and get some work experience, shadowing experience or do some voluntary work.

Work experience and voluntary work are a great way to get a 'hands-on' feel for what a job involves. Don't be afraid to volunteer for several different roles. All work experiences and voluntary work are useful and can have a positive impact on your self-esteem and confidence. It will also demonstrate to potential employers that you have carefully considered your career.

There are different ways of getting work experience or voluntary work:

- Contact an organisation you are interested in e.g. if you are interested in working in the media industry you could contact the BBC Human Resources department directly
- Contact an organisation that will be able to offer advice on work experience and/or voluntary work and in some cases arrange a placement for you
- Check out the local voluntary agency in your area. There are a number of websites you can look at e.g. *http://www.do-it.org.uk/* or *http://www.volunteering.org.uk/*

For help with arranging work experience and voluntary work speak to the careers services locally or, if you have left college or university, ask them directly for help.

See the following websites:

www.disabilitytoolkits.ac.uk
www.careers-scotland.org.uk
www.gowales.co.uk
*https://www.gov.uk/volunteering/
    find-volunteer-placements*
www.voluntaryworker.co.uk/

Internships

Internships/placements offer you the opportunity for a fixed amount of time to gain some training 'on the job'. They can be both paid and voluntary.

They can be useful in helping you decide whether a career/position is right for you while you gain useful skills and experience and get to know a sector of work. They may also lead to a permanent placement in the workplace.

For more information and available internships visit:

http://graduatetalentpool.direct.gov.uk/cms/
   ShowPage/Home_page/p!ccaacfg
http://faststream.civilservice.gov.uk/
   summer-diversity-internships/
www.milkround.com

Apprenticeships

For more information on potential schemes in your area if you are in the UK:

http://www.apprenticeships.org.uk/employers.aspx

Additional skills and training

Training never stops. When you have found a career which offers you the opportunity to pursue your interests and take advantage of your strengths and skills, it is important to consider what additional training may be required to progress.

The following sites have some good advice and tips on what training or qualifications may be needed for different roles:

www.careerswales.com
www.disabilitytoolkits.ac.uk
www.careers-scotland.org.uk
www.nextstep.org.uk
www.monster.co.uk
www.jobs.nhs.uk/advice/intro.html
www.learndirect.co.uk

CHAPTER 4

Finding a job and gaining support

This chapter is designed to give you all the help and advice you need about preparing for the workplace. This includes looking for jobs and the process of applying. It is aimed at the potential employee.

Finding your way through the system can be hard to do. Knowing what systems are out there to help and what specialised support is available can seem like walking through a maze and meeting dead ends along the way. It can feel exhausting and bewildering. Don't do this alone. If there is uncertainty about the process of finding a job, do ask for help. There are government systems, careers guidance organisations, recruitment agencies and help from school, college or university there to assist you. This chapter provides some information on these processes and places where information and support can be provided. If you have difficulties with communication, or anxiety about making a call, someone can do this on your behalf (you may need to give written consent in an email or letter).

Who can help you?

One of the first places to go if you have a recognised disability in the UK is to contact JobCentre Plus. There is specialist support available for you there in the form of the Disability Employment Advisers (DEAs). Disability Employment Advisers are there to help find suitable employment and to help plan the most effective way to get into and keep a job.

The DEA can also refer to a Supported Employment Agency (see below for further details), if appropriate, to assist in preparation for a job and will help to find a work placement or further training. Go to your local JobCentre and ask them how to contact the DEA for further assistance.

Disability-friendly employers

Some organisations advertising jobs have a 'positive attitude towards applications from disabled people' by employing the 'two ticks' symbol. This does not mean that other organisations do not have a positive attitude! It simply means that the organisation is particularly keen to overcome any barriers a person with a disability may face during the application process. Look out for the 'two ticks' symbol when searching for jobs at Jobcentre Plus.

Specifically disability-friendly jobs may be found on these websites:

www.jobability.org
https://www.gov.uk/browse/disabilities

Recruitment agencies

If you don't know where to look and how to apply recruitment agencies can help to match your skills and qualifications to their available jobs. There are many general agencies, but often they specialise in a work area e.g. technical, call centre work, administration. Other forms of recruitment agencies e.g. temping agencies (which help you find temporary jobs) are also a useful resource. Temping can lead to a permanent position and offers a good opportunity for you to try different roles. Recruitment and temping agencies are a good option if you find the interview process particularly challenging. The agency themselves will conduct an informal interview and any relevant assessments rather than you having to attend several different interviews.

There are also some specialist agencies that assist people with a disability.

Specialist recruitment agencies
Specialist agencies usually have knowledge about the sector and how to support someone with some additional needs and may be able to advise you whether they have services and jobs in your area.

They often have good relationships with national and local employers and can prepare the person for the interview and the job. They can also provide support once placed.

Equal Approach is a specialist recruitment agency

http://equalapproach.com/

Remploy is a specialist service provider

http://www.remploy.co.uk/employment-services.ashx

Prospects is a part of the National Autistic Society

http://www.autism.org.uk/prospects

Supported employment

Supported Employment Agencies can help you if you are unemployed and have a disability or health condition and want to return to, or start work. They will support you in a job, offer you training and advice, as well as help you to find a suitable position. The government pays these supported employment organisations to help people get into employment and off benefits.

If you have a disability or a health condition and are struggling to find a job it may be worth using the services of a Supported Employment Agency. The Disability Employment Adviser at your local

Jobcentre Plus will be able to advise you of local agencies and refer you to them. Two examples are:

www.remploy.co.uk
www.shaw-trust.org.uk

There are also some specialist supported employment services such as:

http://www.autism.org.uk/our-services/
employment-support/employees.aspx

Job searching tips

Finding a job may require several different approaches to be successful, especially when jobs are in short supply. Leaving school, college or university and looking for a full or part-time job can be daunting for everyone and especially so if you have had some challenges in learning and may lack confidence in some skills. Having an action plan and being organised can considerably increase your chances of being successful.

- **Look in local papers** – there are sometimes set days for advertising specific jobs, find these out from reading papers in your local library or going online.
- **Ask friends and family** if they know of anyone looking for someone – networking is a great way to tell others you are looking. They may not know someone now but if something

occurs there is a greater chance of being approached.

- **Drop your CV in** to shops and offices – keep it to two pages maximum on one sheet of paper.
- **Tell people you meet socially** that you are looking for a job (i.e. if it is an appropriate moment, such as if you are in a shared conversation talking about jobs and work).
- Check there are no jobs in the university or college, if you have recently left. Sometimes there are part-time or temporary jobs helping out at events or open days. Voluntary work is useful and can be added to your CV. This may lead to a job, shows others you are interested and willing and gives you transferable skills.
- Don't have a too fixed a view about what you want to do to begin with. This is especially true when there is a shortage of jobs. Getting one job may lead you into other opportunities and at a minimum allows you to have something to discuss in the interview and some potentially transferable skills.

https://www.gov.uk/looking-for-work-if-disabled/looking-for-a-job

- In the UK, speak to the Disability Employment Adviser at the local JobCentre. They can refer you to a specialist work psychologist, if appropriate, or carry out an 'employment assessment', asking you about skills and experience and what kind of roles you are looking for.

- Sector-specific jobsites (e.g. to work for a charity (*http://jobs.thirdsector.co.uk*) or if you want to work in catering (*www.caterer.com*))

Narrowing the choices

When you find a job that you are interested in, take down the details (by hand, by saving to a computer or by printing them out) but don't just stop at one job. Look and see if there are several.

Check the deadline for an application hasn't passed.

Create a shortlist of jobs you are interested in to look at in closer detail.

Be realistic in terms of applying; don't try and apply for too many at once as you need to amend your CV to suit the job and write a specific cover letter relating to the application.

If you are not sure which to go for discuss it with someone you trust such as a tutor, parent or careers adviser.

From your shortlist, choose which ones suit your skills and experience best and apply for them.

Then:

- Look at the deadline for the application so you know how long you have to get everything ready. Enter this in your phone or diary, with reminders.
- What is required of you? e.g. completing an online application; taking a test online;

undergoing an interview (or more than one); doing some specific tasks; making a presentation; taking a portfolio of your work?

- Do you need a handwritten or typed cover letter?
- Can you email or post it, or are you able to drop it in?
- Have you the right size envelope to put the documents in? Think about sending the documents by recorded post if they have certificates in them.
- Do you need to book time off work if you are in another job? What will you tell your present boss? Have you holiday leave you can take so you can attend the interview?
- Do you need to practise completing the form so there are no crossings out or spelling errors? Can someone check it through with you?
- Do you want to disclose your difficulties at this point? Is there a box to tick?
- What adjustments may you need in the interview e.g. extra time, a quiet setting, use of a computer?
- If you need to travel have you the money to do so? Do you know how to get to the place and back?
- Do you need someone to come with you and to be there during the interview e.g. if you have communication difficulties?

Completing an application form

Here are some tips.

The basics

Look at the job advert; what does it ask you to do? For example, does it ask you to:

Apply online?
Request a paper form through the post?
Complete an electronic copy of the form?
When is the deadline?

What is needed to complete the application form – for example, a computer with internet access, qualification certificates and/or your National Insurance number, two references?

Read the instructions for completion carefully. For example they may ask you to complete the form using CAPITAL letters or a **black** pen. They may ask you to ignore certain questions for the particular job you are applying for.

If you have a paper form to complete photocopy it to practise on and save the original form for your final draft.

The form

Standard information is usually required for most applications, including information on job history (where you may have worked before, what the role was etc.) and educational history, skills and qualifications and some information about you (where you live, hobbies and interests).

Do try to tailor the section about interests and experiences to the specific job you are applying for.

Read and have to hand the job description, person specification and any other information on the organisation when completing the form to ensure that you are selling yourself in a way that meets the criteria outlined for the role – answer each aspect of this.

Recognise that the skills from working in one position or from life experience may be transferable to the demands of the job you are applying for e.g.

If you're a parent you may have transferable time management and organisation skills from getting your children ready for school on time.

You may also have money management skills from managing your own finances.

If you have travelled with others you may have experiences that demonstrate team working, planning and time management skills.

See Chapter 3 for more on transferable skills.

For more detailed information on completing an application form visit:

https://nationalcareersservice.direct.gov.uk/ advice/getajob/applications/Pages/default.aspx
http://www.prospects.ac.uk/applying_for_jobs.htm

http://www.wikihow.com/
Fill-Out-Job-Application-Forms

References

Employers will want at least one referee to provide a reference for you. The names, addresses and occupations for any referees will need to be listed – you may need both personal and professional references, for example from a teacher, someone you have done voluntary work with, family friend or employer.

Always ask the person/s you plan to use as a referee whether they are willing to provide a reference for you before submitting your application.

Submitting

Once the application form has been completed, read through it and ask someone else to read through it to make sure there are no spelling errors or general mistakes.

If it is a paper form, photocopy the form to keep a record of what has been said.

If the form has been completed using a computer, save an electronic copy in a folder on the computer.

Once submitted, it is good practice to phone the number given on the job advert to check that they have received your application form.

Writing a Curriculum Vitae (CV)

A CV is your chance to sell yourself to potential employers. The employer will have many CVs to look through and will look for something that stands out and fits the job description.

Here are some hints and tips to help.

There is no universally accepted format; however a CV should be:

A well-presented document
A source of interesting, relevant information
A document that sells your skills
Honest and factual.

- A CV should be ideally no more than two pages long. It is not a life story! It's a sales tool to get an interview.
- The first 20 words should make the person reading it see what your skills are (not your qualifications).
- Personal contact details should be clearly presented for the reader to contact you e.g. email address, phone number and home address.

It is important to recognise that the skills you may already have from working in one position or from life experience may be transferable to the demands of the job you are applying for e.g. money management skills from managing your own finances, or working in a bar may have given you experience of dealing with customers and having good communication skills, travelling independently may have developed your planning and organisational skills.

- Describe skills and give examples to demonstrate them.
- Describe lessons learnt in another job or in work experience, and how you can apply this learning to another setting.
- How do you show how you have gone 'the extra mile', i.e. done extra or more than was expected of you in another setting.

Don't just give personality descriptors, but focus on achievements and outcomes, e.g. 'as a consequence of me doing X, Y was achieved'. BUT don't over exaggerate or lie.

- Under hobbies and interests, try to think about something that is related to the job or something that will make you stand out from other people.
- The names and contact details of two referees should be provided at the end of your CV. Always ask the people you intend to use as referees if they are willing to provide you with a reference before submitting your CV.

What not to have in your CV

- Lies
- Spelling errors – if you find spelling, writing and proofing your work hard, then have someone check the document before submitting it
- Crossings out – this looks untidy and does not look to the potential employer as though you care very much
- Sending out a standard cover letter to everyone and not bothering to make it relevant to the job description or company – the employer wants to know why you are suitable for the job, and does not want a 'generic' CV that has been sent out to everyone
- Don't make it longer than two pages if you can.

CV help including templates and examples

For more advice, examples and templates have a look at the following:

www.prospects.ac.uk/cv_content.htm
www.kent.ac.uk/careers/cv/cvexamples.htmhttp://
www.businessballs.com/curriculum.htm
http://cv.monster.co.uk

Alternative CVs

If writing a CV is too hard for you and you could represent yourself in a different way, there is an increasing trend to create video CVs filming yourself talking about what you can do, have done, and would be able to do in the job you are applying for.

Make sure the format it has been made in can be opened by others.

https://nationalcareersservice.direct.gov.uk/
advice/getajob/cvs/Pages/cvalterative.aspx
http://www.totaljobs.com/careers-advice/
cvs-and-applications/how-to-make-a-video-cv

Writing a covering letter

CVs should be accompanied by a covering letter unless indicated otherwise.

Why write a cover letter?

The cover letter is the FIRST THING a potential employer will look at and is therefore very important. It forms the basis for a potential employer's first impressions of the applicant. It will influence whether they want to find out more about you and to read the CV.

It's a chance to market yourself to the organisation and show how you meet the specific criteria outlined in the job description and person specification – it tells them why they should interview YOU.

A covering letter should usually be no longer than one A4 page.

Further help with covering letters

https://nationalcareersservice.direct.gov.uk/advice/
getajob/cvs/Pages/writeacoveringletter.aspx

http://www.prospects.ac.uk/covering_letters.htm
http://www.kent.ac.uk/careers/cv/
   coveringletters.htm
http://www.jobsite.co.uk/worklife/
   how-to-write-a-cover-letter-10765/

CHAPTER 5

Interviews – from beginning to end

This chapter covers each of the stages before, during and after the interview process.

New beginnings

A new job offers everyone new opportunities to 're-invent' themselves and be the person they want to be (or want others to think of them as) rather than the way others may have seen them in the past. (However, this of course does not mean lying about who you are or what you have done). Individuals with the conditions described in this book may sometimes find that being organised can be harder to do, or it may cause feelings of anxiety going into an unfamiliar setting. By planning each of the stages from pre-interview to post-interview reflection, there is a greater chance of success, and less risk of raised anxiety levels affecting performance on the day.

Disclosure

There are many different issues to be considered when contemplating when to disclose a Specific Learning Difficulty (SpLD).

Consider:

- **What you are disclosing –** are you going to describe your challenges as a disability with a label or diagnosis or are you going to say some things are a little harder for you? What language do you use to do this? What form of information do you give this in – orally, or showing a written report?
- **Who you disclose to –** who do you want to know in the workplace that you have some challenges and who don't you want to tell? Think about this as your line manager may ask you about who to disclose to.
- **When you disclose** (if ever) will depend very much on your individual difficulties and circumstances. Do you say something when applying for a job on the application form? Do you say something in the interview? Do you say something if you get the job? Do you wait till there are problems arising before you tell.

Think carefully about whether you feel there are adjustments that can be made to aid you in the position you are applying for. If your difficulties aren't obvious and you are unsure whether you will need any adjustments to fulfil the role, you may want to wait until you know who within the organisation you should talk to about needing a workplace adjustment (e.g. someone in Human Resources, a colleague or your manager).

But also remember that your employer cannot support you unless they know you have some challenges. Telling them once you are having problems makes it much harder for them to make any reasonable adjustments for you.

Stages in the interview process

One to two weeks before the interview

This is the time to do the background preparatory work.

- Gather together any information you need to take with you e.g. certificates, identification, copy of your CV and place all in a folder ready.
- This is the time to find out about the potential employer and company you are aiming to work at whether this is in a public, private or voluntary setting. Go on the company website and read through what they do.
- If you are disclosing your difficulties, find out about the format of the interview so you can consider with the employer what adjustments are required or the need to use Access to Work to provide guidance and assistance e.g. you may want to ask for: a quiet room for an assessment; additional time if unfamiliar task; one-to-one assessment rather than group;

bringing along an assistant to aid
communication.

- If a presentation is required, then this is the
time to prepare and practise. If there is a time
limit for it, make sure this is stuck to. Make
sure your presentation is in line with what you
have been asked to do if a title has been
given. Let someone else hear the presentation
as well and give feedback if possible. Ask
them how you appear e.g. friendly, engaging,
tone of voice is interesting or boring/
monotone.
- Have a look on Google Maps where the address
of the interview is if this is unfamiliar to you.
- Make sure you have read the job description
and have examples of how you can meet the
skills the company requires. Do you understand
what is being asked of you? If you are not sure,
go through it with someone before the interview
so you can appear confident.
- Be prepared to describe any of your challenges
in a positive way ... "I have xx but I have
overcome some of these challenges by yy. I
would be good at this job because of zz".
- Prepare some questions you can ask the
interviewers about what the job entails.
- If you are not sure how you sound to others,
practise answering questions beforehand and
ask for feedback. Listen to what friends and
family are telling you – it could help you to get
the job. Ask them to say what your expression
on your face is like. You may think you are

being friendly but be coming across to others as aggressive or sullen.

- If you are not sure what will happen at the interview phone or email the company (there will be contact details on the letter inviting you for an interview) and ask to speak to the HR(Human Resources) manager or department (depending on the size of the company).
- Organise a 'mock' interview:

  ○ Ask someone if they can interview you
  ○ Give them the job description
  ○ Talk to them about the job and the workplace you have applied to
  ○ Get them to try and ask you the difficult questions – write them down so you can give them to the person to go through.

Preparing the night before

Read through the directions to get to the place the night before so you know where you need to go, and make sure you have the correct money for the journey.

- Check the time of the interview and the address once again so departure time can be worked out.
- Get out clothes ready the night before. Are they clean?
- Think what is the appropriate clothing for the interview – it is usually better to look more

formal than less so e.g. black or grey trousers/skirt and a white or pale coloured striped or plain shirt or blouse. Have clean and polished shoes.

- Check the weather, if it's going to rain or snow then an early start, a warm coat or an umbrella may be needed.
- If you wear tights, do you have a spare pair just in case they get laddered on the way?
- Go through your presentation if one is to be made. Have you got this saved on a USB? Make sure it is in your bag.

http://career-advice.monster.com/job-interview/interview-appearance/jobs.aspx

On the day

- Make sure you are showered, have clean teeth and smell clean! Wear some deodorant – when nervous we can all sweat more.
- Have some breakfast so you don't feel faint and you can focus on your interview.
- Remember to take medication if normally taken (e.g. ADHD medication), especially as concentrating and listening is important today!
- Leave additional time for the journey, just in case of delays or disruption in transport. It's better to be there early and go and have a coffee or drink in a café. It also gives you time to use the toilet!

Arriving at the interview

There is a lot of truth in the old saying: 'You only have one chance to make a good first impression'.

Studies have shown that within four minutes of you meeting someone they will have formed judgments about you and that these judgments will inform their subsequent impressions, so it is important to make the most of the first crucial minutes.

- It is worth remembering that even before going into the interview; you will probably be under observation by reception staff. Be courteous to everyone you meet. In some businesses they ask other team members for their comments about you and how you behaved.
- Go to the toilet when you arrive and check your appearance including your hair. Is your shirt or blouse tucked in? Are all buttons and zips done up that should be?
- Start off with a confident smile and a firm handshake. Practise this with someone else beforehand to make sure your smile is not making you look sinister, and your handshake is firm but not gripping the other person so tight that they want to cry!
- When introducing yourself be pleasant, polite and business like – avoid saying things like 'Hiya mate', better to say 'Good morning' or 'Good afternoon' etc. depending on the time of day.

- This doesn't mean that if you are very nervous or appear so that you've failed. Try to remain calm. Slow deep breaths. Remember everyone feels nervous. You can say so, to the interviewer if you feel it is really affecting your performance.

In the interview

How you appear to others

What you say is crucial to the success of your interview, but how you say it is also important. How you look, and act and sound can be important in the first few minutes of an interview.

- Think about the non-verbal signals (how you are sitting, your actions and not just the words) that you are giving – are you sounding interested and enthusiastic or as though you can't really be bothered? Be sincere and show you are really interested in the job you are applying for.
- Think about your seating position when you are asked to sit. Usually the best approach is to sit reasonably upright but sitting back into the chair, and it sometimes helps you to feel more relaxed if you sit at a very slight angle to the interviewer rather than face on. If you are fidgety then try to have your hands clasped together and in your lap. If you have to, sit on them!

- Crossing your arms and legs can make you appear defensive. Leaning too far forward could be interpreted as an aggressive stance, and slouching or leaning too far back in the chair may give the impression to the interviewer that you don't care too much about the interview.
- Avoid any personal idiosyncrasies, such as fiddling with your clothing or jewellery.
- Using your hands when you talk is perfectly acceptable as they can often bring a conversation to life. Avoid pointing or waggling your finger at the interviewer to make your point!
- Eye contact is essential in conveying interest. Lack of direct eye contact is sometimes interpreted as the interviewee being insincere and untrustworthy, even though it may be from shyness. Maintaining eye contact also helps you to gauge the interviewer's reaction to what you have to say, and whether you should expand your answer or be more succinct. If you are not sure how much to look, you could look at the questioner's ear rather than appearing to stare at them.
- If there are several people interviewing you, then eye contact may become more difficult, but it is usual to look at the person asking each question while acknowledging the others with a glance from time to time.
- Show you are listening. It is okay to take a few notes if the questions are lengthy, or if you need to remind yourself of something you want to stress.

- If you are not sure what has been asked, say so and ask for it to be repeated. This is fine to do so. If you really don't understand what has been asked of you, then don't respond with any answer. You could say: 'Sorry, I am not quite sure what you are asking me, could you explain this to me perhaps in a slightly different way possibly?'.
- The tone of your voice can also indicate to others whether you sound interested or sound bored. A monotonal voice can sound flat and boring to others. Ask others if you are not sure what you sound like or tape your voice and play it back.

Selling yourself
When answering questions you will need to address what is being asked of you while answering all questions in the most positive way to sell yourself. Listen to the question. If you need to, write it down.

- You will usually be asked 'tell me something about yourself' to start to get you talking. Be prepared with a two minute response to this beforehand.
- You need to demonstrate your knowledge of the job, the organisation and yourself.
- Make sure you have read through the job description – have specific examples prepared of what you have done to show how you could meet the criteria.
- Be prepared to talk about your strengths. You can do this by saying: 'I used to do x but now I can do y'.

- Consider how you may disclose your difficulties – present them in a positive light in terms of how you have overcome some challenges and the way you have done so.
- You can talk about specific needs for training if there are gaps in your skills – no-one is perfect!
- Do have concrete, i.e. real, examples to show your skills and experiences, 'I am a good team player', for example. 'I have always played team games and at university I was captain of the football team' or 'I am very meticulous in what I do, for example, at college I was one of the first to create a website using the code we were being taught'.

When asking a potential candidate questions the interviewers are trying to establish the following:

- Does the applicant have the ability to complete the job?
- In what areas is he or she weak? How will the weaknesses affect their performance?
- What are his or her ambitions?
- What kind of a person is this?
- Does she or he have growth potential?
- Should this person get an offer?

You should not lie in an interview, but at the same time, you do not need to tell the employer every detail of your life. If you are uncertain what to say and how to say it talk to someone you trust.

Answering the employer's questions

Remember that not all interviewers are experienced or well trained, and they too can be nervous. However, they will be the ones asking you the questions.

It is your responsibility to ensure that you convey your suitability for the job. With good preparation you will be able to do this.

Some basic rules

- Listen carefully to the question you are being asked.
- If you are not sure what has been asked, seek clarification, ask them politely to repeat the question.
- Be careful not to talk over your interviewer but leave space for him or her to respond.
- Better to give short answers and ask if they wish you to go into more detail.

The following points may help:

- **Remember that honesty is the best policy.** Admitting, for example, to a period of poor motivation shows more integrity than blaming someone else for a poor grade or poor performance. It is better to present past actions positively as learning experiences rather than cover them up. Although you have an obligation to tell the truth in an interview, you do not have to tell your whole life story.

Try to give the relevant parts associated with this post.

- **Be prepared to talk.** Avoid yes/no answers and expand on the answer. Take your cue from the interviewer, and if you are not sure that they have heard enough ask, 'Would you like me to continue?'
- **Try not to talk too quickly.** When nervous we can rush answers and it can sound as though you are 'gabbling'.
- **Ask for clarification** if you need it; this will help you to answer the question more effectively and also demonstrates confidence and control.
- **Pause if you need to.** If you need a moment to think before answering a particularly difficult question it is acceptable to pause or ask for time to think about the question. This is better than saying the first thing that comes into your head.
- **Be enthusiastic.** Interviewers like to see enthusiasm but do not expect a perfect performance. If you make a mistake it is not the end of the world; try to forget it and move on.
- **Don't try to fill silences** left by the interviewers. Silences are rarely as long as they feel at the time, and whether the interviewer is simply gathering their thoughts or, more deliberately, checking your reactions, it is up to you how much and what you say.

Dealing with difficult questions
The interviewer may try to ask you some less obvious questions to find out more about yourself. Some questions, which can be perceived as particularly difficult include those which appear to be an invitation to express all your negative qualities, such as:

- What do you think is your biggest weakness?
- What would you say has been your greatest failure?

They may also ask you some questions, which require you to think about yourself in a different way. These might include:

- How would your friends describe you?
- Why is this job important to you?

Listen to the first question here ... how would **your** friends ... not how would you ... be careful to listen to what is **actually** being asked.

Sometimes these questions are asked to see how you will react and to see whether you are listening. The rules for answering these are the same as for any other question: relax, be honest, keep in mind the points that you want to make about yourself, and emphasise the positive while minimising weaker areas. If you don't know an answer then say so, rather than trying to make something up.

The first question: What do you think is your biggest weakness?

Someone might answer the first question by saying that their strengths lie in their ability to think problems through clearly, and that they can sometimes be frustrated with people who don't work logically, though they have learnt to appreciate the different insights that they can bring to a class project. This outlines a weakness but stresses their strengths and their ability to learn from their mistakes.

The second question: What would you say has been your greatest failure?

When talking about a failed examination or an unsuccessful project explain what positive lessons you have learnt from it, and try to highlight how these might be relevant to the present application.

The third question: How would your friends describe you?

This focuses on your relationships with other people, particularly those close to you. Your answer could cover your loyalty, your understanding or your readiness to help, e.g. 'I think that my friends would say ...' or, 'I hope that my friends would say ... '.

The fourth question: Why is this job important to you?

Your response should portray some information about your principles, aims and ambitions in life.

Have a go at answering some of these questions and try these virtual interviews:

http://career-advice.monster.co.uk/job-interview/
   careers.aspx
http://www.jobinterviewquestions.org/
   interview-questions-and-answers/
http://www.bbc.co.uk/northernireland/schools/
   11_16/gogetit/getthatjob/interviewgame.shtml
http://www.telegraph.co.uk/finance/jobs/
   10104103/25-tough-interview-questions.html

Think of some questions you may like to ask your interview panel; information you have gathered about the organisation and information in the job description may help.
   For advice on what to ask your interviewer visit:

http://career-advice.monster.co.uk/job-
   interview/job-interview-questions/questions-to-
   ask-your-interviewer-video-advice/article.aspx

Practise using the **STAR** strategy to answer questions:

http://www.quintcareers.com/STAR_interviewing.
   html

Positive endings

This is the chance to ask those questions you prepared before attending the interview. If you are not given the opportunity to ask questions, assert yourself politely by saying you have a number of questions or points to raise and ask if this is the appropriate time to do so.

Once the interview is at an end, if the employers have not already made the next step clear in terms of when they expect to let you know the outcome, ask them.

It is important to end the interview on a positive note. Thank the interviewers for their time and the opportunity to speak with them. Shake their hands if offered.

After the interview

If you haven't heard from the interviewer within the time frame indicated at the close of the interview, call them. Ask if they have made their final decision and if not confirm that you're still interested in the job and ask when they plan to make a decision.

If you have not been successful ask for feedback so that you can get any pointers on what to improve before another interview. Thank them for their time. You may be offered a position at a later date.

Discuss with someone close to you what they think you could do better. Practise those skills. Think about whether there are skills gaps? Is there a training need? Is the wrong type of job being applied for? Are you lacking enthusiasm in the interview because of a lack of interest in the post? Is there a need for additional assistance?

Don't be too despondent, and prepare for your next interview. After all, the more interviews you tackle the more polished you become.

CHAPTER 6

In the job

This chapter considers the implications of starting and keeping a job. Everyone feels nervous when starting a job and you will not immediately be expected to know exactly what to do and when.

The first week of work is always hard for anyone:

- Meeting the line manager
- Meeting new colleagues
- Navigating your way around a new setting
- Learning about your new job
- Gaining an understanding about the working environment and the rules.

For an individual with specific challenges the first few weeks in a new job can feel very daunting coping with all these changes. Being prepared helps and this entails understanding what the job description actually and practically means, and gaining an understanding of the workplace culture. Gathering information on this before you start can help, but may not always be possible.

In the job

Getting the beginning right

Where possible arrange a meeting with the line manager and/or Human Resources before starting the job. This can allay some fears and provide information on what is expected to be prepared for the first day. At this meeting:

- Go through the job description and clarify anything that remains unclear including company policies e.g. dress code (if you don't have a uniform to wear); work flow; line management and hierarchy (if working as part of a team); who to go to discuss aspects of the job; what the review and appraisal process is.
- Find out the workplace rules:

  - What people generally do regarding breaks and lunchtimes – how long do they take? Do they go out to get a sandwich or is there a work canteen? Do they go together or one at a time? How often can you break for tea or coffee?
  - At the beginning and end of the day do you need to 'clock in' or verbally tell your line manager you have arrived and are leaving?
  - If you are ill, and can't work, who do you need to tell and how e.g. phoning in or emailing?
  - Use of the internet – can you use it for personal use, are there some restricted sites you are not allowed on?
  - Find out the policy on receiving or sending personal emails.

- o Is there an expectation of what time you are expected to be in, and do you need to clock in?
- o Is there a 'dress down' day i.e. a day when you can be dressed more casually? What does that mean – are there restrictions on the type of clothes on these days as well?

- Are there specific ways of addressing colleagues and managers that you should know about e.g. by their first name or Mr or Mrs XX?
- Are there acronyms (letters that stand for something) specific to the organization. e.g. DOB – **D**ate **O**f **B**irth. If there are, then ask if they can be written down.
- What you should do if there are problems of any sort e.g.

  - o Don't understand what work needs to be completed
  - o Not getting on with peers
  - o Having difficulties with clients or customers
  - o Can't meet a deadline set by others.

- How often will there be a review?
- Discuss the work setting:

  - o Do you work in the same place each day
  - o Is there hot-desking (i.e. use any desk that is free if working in an office setting) and, if so, could this be problematic moving around. Is there a need to be in a regular place?
  - o Is there a locker or a drawer where you can keep your possessions safe?

- Discuss, if you have disclosed, how your disability or challenges affect you and what reasonable adjustments you have found are helpful.
- Discuss if an Access to Work assessment may be of help.

Dress code

If a uniform is provided in the job or a specific dress code stated (e.g. black trousers or skirt and a white shirt) then the dress code is much easier as there is less choice to be made. However, there is still a need to look professional and to show that some care has been taken with appearance.

- Make sure that clothes are clean and ironed, and shoes are, where possible, polished and clean (and you are clean as well).
- If you wear perfume be sensitive to others if they are allergic to certain smells.
- Ensure shirts are tucked in (if they are supposed to be).
- Hair and nails need to be clean.
- If you wear make-up, unless this is related to your job (e.g. work on a make-up counter, stage make-up), it is better to wear less during the day. If you are not sure, have a make-up trial done for you in a department store. Go at a quiet time when there is more likelihood someone will show you what to do. MAC (a name of a cosmetic range) does courses on how to do make-up.

- Avoid clothing that has words on them that could be offensive to others. If you are not sure, then ask. Sports team, university, and fashion brand names on clothing are generally acceptable.

If no uniform or dress code has been stated:

- Look around the work setting and see what others are wearing. See what the line managers are wearing as this shows what to aspire to.
- If casual wear is indicated, this does not mean not bothering at all.
- Better to be the best dressed person rather than the sloppiest one!
- Keeping to one or two colours apart from black, navy, beige or white as neutral colours usually works best.
- Usually shorts, track pants, and leggings, and in some places jeans, are not acceptable.
- Avoid showing too much skin e.g.if female, too short a top or too open.
- If wearing a skirt or dress be aware of how short it is when sitting down.
- Some places do not like their staff to wear flip flops, or trainers. You may want to check on this as well.
- If you have piercings check whether they need to be removed for work, or if you have tattoos whether they need to be covered up.

http://humanresources.about.com/od/
   workrelationships/tp/dress_code_collect.htm

Workplace etiquette and customs

Getting along with people appropriately in the workplace is essential to your well-being and success in work. There are unwritten rules about how to communicate with different parties in the workplace. Here are some hints and tips to help.

Communicating with your boss/manager/ HR department:

An individual's relationship with their line manager is very different from a student's relationship with their lecturer or with a teacher in school. You need to find out how to address them.

- Ask your line manager when you start your job how they want to be addressed e.g. by their first name.
- Avoid asking personal questions about someone's family/personal life unless s/he volunteers this information.
- Think about when you send emails and the number of emails you are sending to ask for help.
- If you want to have a conversation about your work, ask when it will be most convenient to do so.
- Use formal language (e.g. 'Excuse me, when is the deadline for this piece of work?'). There are accepted ways of behaving in certain situations, for example, when taking part in meetings, raise your hand slightly and/or make eye contact with the person leading the meeting before you speak.

- Don't interrupt – wait for your boss/manager to finish speaking before you answer or ask your question.

For further advice on communicating with your boss/manager:

http://career-advice.monster.co.uk/in-the-workplace/workplace-issues/how-can-i-manage-my-manager/article.aspx

For advice on working under different managers/bosses:

http://career-advice.monster.co.uk/in-the-workplace/workplace-issues/how-can-i-work-effectively-under-multiple-bosses/article.aspx

Communicating with colleagues/co-workers
When first meeting co-workers/colleagues:

- Be friendly and introduce yourself. It is fine to be a little nervous.
- Ask them some questions about the job if they are doing something similar but don't keep asking unless someone has said this is fine to do.
- Wait for them to talk with you and be polite.
- Don't discuss any personal issues or views with your colleagues especially about your line manager as s/he could hear of this and you could be in trouble.

- Try and watch how others are behaving in your office or workplace setting.

Working day-to-day with co-workers

- Understanding who is a work colleague and who at work is also a friend can be difficult to work out. Just because you work with someone every day it does not necessarily mean they are your friend.
- Try to recognise signs of friendship. One of these may be if someone asks you to go for a drink or to go out socially.
- In discussion and when talking with colleagues it is usually not a good idea for one person to dominate the conversation even if they are the ones who may have the answers:

  - Use more informal language (e.g. 'When do we have to finish this piece of work by?')
  - You can interrupt when there is a lull in the conversation.

- Don't forward 'funny' emails with jokes to everyone in work. What is funny to you may not be to others.

For advice on how to resolve conflict with colleagues:

http://career-advice.monster.co.uk/in-the-workplace/workplace-issues/how-do-i-resolve-conflict-with-a-colleague/article.aspx

For advice on how to improve relationships with colleagues:

> *http://career-advice.monster.co.uk/in-the-workplace/workplace-issues/how-to-be-a-better-co-worker-video-advice/article.aspx*

For advice on the unwritten rules of the workplace, useful books:

The Hidden Curriculum of Getting and Keeping a Job: Navigating the Social Landscape of Employment.

A Guide for Individuals with Autism Spectrum and Other Social-Cognitive Challenges.

Other forms of communication

Email etiquette

There are lots of ways you can go wrong when sending an email in work, that can have effects not only for the individual but also for the organisation.

Some key rules to consider are as follows:

- Be polite and be aware that others may read the email and they can be kept
- Be concise and to the point
- Try to use proper spelling, grammar and punctuation. Use proofing software if needed
- Create a template for frequently used responses
- Do not attach unnecessary files

- Remember to add greetings and a signature to your email
- Do not overuse the high priority option on an email
- Do not write in CAPITALS
- **Always** read the email before you send it
- Do not overuse 'Reply to All'
- Take care with abbreviations and emoticons
- Do NOT forward chain letters
- Do not copy a message or attachment without permission
- Do not use email to discuss confidential information
- Make sure the subject heading is related to the content
- Don't send or forward emails containing libelous, defamatory, offensive, racist or obscene remarks
- Don't forward virus hoaxes and chain letters
- Keep your language gender neutral
- Don't reply to spam
- Use cc: field sparingly.

Further advice see the link below:

http://office.microsoft.com/en-us/outlook-help/ 12-tips-for-better-email-etiquette-HA001205410.aspx

Phone etiquette

- Focus on the call, and do not be distracted by other people around you

- Smile if you are trying to be positive, it can help you to sound positive
- Be professional if this is a work call. You are representing the company
- Identify yourself and give your name
- Stay calm, if this is difficult, ask to call back
- If nervous, have some notes in front of you to assist you
- Do not ask the person personal details unless this is a part of your role
- If uncertain how to behave, speak to the line manager and ask to be shown what to do.

http://www.wikihow.com/Answer-the-Phone-Politely

Good customer/client service

Most jobs will require some element of working with a customer or client. Good customer/client service benefits not only the customer but also the company and your career. Working with customers/clients is not always easy.

- Try to think like the customer; ask yourself how you would like to be treated and what information would be useful for them.
- Approach all customers with a smile, even if you are feeling grumpy on the inside! A happy, approachable face can make all the difference to the quality of customer interaction, especially if the customer is dissatisfied.
- You may have heard the saying 'the customer is

always right' – obviously this is not exactly true; it is referring to the attitude you should take when dealing with customers. For example, it may mean that you apologise for things that may not be your fault, as when a customer has had to wait for your service. Apologising shows the customer that you understand where their complaint is coming from.

- Some people you meet may also have additional challenges e.g. slower to process information, difficulties with writing or communicating. Treat others in the way you wish to be treated yourself, with respect and patience.
- If you feel you are unable to help the customer/client or feel that they are behaving aggressively it is okay to ask for help either from a colleague or manager. Explain what you are going to do, for example, 'If you could bear with me just a minute while I ask a colleague/manager if they might be better able to help you'.

Talking to others e.g. making presentations to peers or others

Not all jobs require individuals to give presentations or talks to others, but if you are in sales or training, or work as part of a team you may have to give a presentation.

Some people find this quite hard to do and it can

make them feel anxious beforehand and while doing it; particularly if they lack experience. This is especially true if communication skills are not a strength or reading notes aloud is harder to do.

Tips to improve a presentation:

- Be prepared. Have notes, and read these through beforehand so the content and key points are clear. Take time to practise, so the presentation fits into the time span allotted.
- Rehearse. Time how long it takes. Do keep to time, it is annoying to others if you run over and it will affect others if they are to follow you.
- Practise in front of someone else – get them to ask some questions so responses are prepared.
- Look at the people you are presenting to, or focus on something they are wearing.
- Don't speak too fast – it is harder for others to listen to you. Better to be slower than not understood at all. Take a slow deep breath before starting.
- Use a computer program such as PowerPoint or Keynote to lay out the information.

- *http://www.wikihow.com/ Create-a-PowerPoint-Presentation*
- *http://www.apple.com/uk/iwork/keynote/*
  - Don't have too many words on every slide – 4 or 5 points per slide are plenty.
  - Use easier to read fonts such as Arial, Verdana.

- ○ Better to keep the design simple so everyone is listening to. Too dark text on a dark background may be harder for someone to read.
- ○ Try to make the presentation flow from one slide to another so colleagues, or those you are communicating with, can follow the topic easily.

Changing times

No organisation stays stationary and there will always be times of change. If you have a hidden impairment such as ASD or Dyspraxia then any change can increase anxiety levels as it may mean learning a new set of skills, or others having higher expectations of you.

Discuss with the line manager the need to know (where possible) when changes may be taking place which are related to the job e.g. someone on leave, change in line management, change in work setting or policies.

If the job changes, then ask for a similar review process as was undertaken as a part of induction when starting the job, as new skills and training may be required.

Talk to someone you feel you can confide in if the changes are causing additional stress.

There will always be a settling down period i.e. a period of time to become accustomed to new working practices, so allow this to happen. This may take several months.

Being aware of general health and well-being at times of change is important as this may assist with reducing the level of anxiety e.g. taking regular exercise and having adequate sleep.

If things go wrong

Mistakes can be made in any job. It is often not the mistake that is the problem but not addressing the consequences of it. If a mistake or error has been made, tell your line manager and discuss the implications of it as soon as possible rather than delaying it or hiding it.

Was this a one-off action or situation, or is there a need for training or support?

What was the reason for it? Try to work this out

e.g. poor planning, impulsivity, lack of understanding, not recognising someone else's feelings, misreading or misspelling a document? Not wanting to ask for help? Have you asked for help before and been snubbed by a peer or manager? Frightened of showing a lack of skills in an area of work? Fear of losing your job?

Burying problems usually means they either happen again and increase the likelihood of consequences for the individual or affect the individual in some way e.g. worrying, affecting sleep, and/or affecting work and relationships.

If repeated mistakes are made, then a review with the line manager is essential to see whether a) the job is the right one or b) can reasonable adjustments be put in place and c) are there health issues e.g. anxiety or depression which need to be addressed first?

For some individuals, it may be the job is not the right one and does not work with the strengths of the individual but just exposes the weaknesses. This can result in lowered self-esteem and a loss of confidence. Sometimes there is a need to accept that a different job may just be a better fit.

Telling lies, intentionally or not (or hiding the truth) is a real problem, even if it was not meant to be intentional. Hiding things from others who may be able to help makes it harder for them to be supportive.

Losing jobs but pretending you are still there

Several examples of pretending a job exists when it doesn't have been described by parents and by individuals. One example of this was where the individual would 'pretend' to family and friends they were still in their job despite them losing it several months before. One individual even left home each morning 'going to work' and would spend the day in the library returning home again in the evening. Another individual became homeless but avoided letting parents know until there was a desperate situation requiring much more support than if they had been able to help earlier on. Avoiding this situation is preferable as regaining trust can be difficult once this has happened.

Bullying and harassment in the workplace

Sadly, this is not uncommon in the workplace. If there is bullying, talk to Human Resources or the line manager. No-one should tolerate this and support and guidance is available. It can be very traumatic especially if someone was also bullied in school as it can recall many feelings perhaps hidden since childhood. Confidence and communication skills training may be worth considering to enhance the way that situations can be dealt with in the future.

https://www.gov.uk/workplace-bullying-and-harassment

ACAS publish a booklet which can be downloaded for employees called:

Bullying and harassment at work: Guidance for employees

http://www.acas.org.uk/index.aspx?articleid=797

CHAPTER 7

Being organised IN work

This chapter provides you with lots of advice that will help with organising the work setting. It is mainly aimed at the employee.

Organisational skills need to be practised and put in place for them to be remembered and used. Just waiting to be organised is not likely to happen and there has to be proactivity. There is increasing evidence that individuals with Specific Learning Difficulties have an increased chance of having organisation, time management and prioritisation challenges. These are called 'executive functioning difficulties'. Understanding this can be a problem but is important because the impact on you and others if time management or self-organisation is poor can result in problems completing work to time, and ultimately holding onto a job.

In order to use your time efficiently and effectively you need to plan ahead and have routines in place as much as possible. The more that skills are routine and automated, the less cognitive load there is having to 'remember to remember' everything.

If there is uncertainty about how to get organised ask the line manager, and consider an Access to Work assessment.

Organising the workspace

Whatever the job, having the work space organised can save time and effort. This may be a car or van, an office desk or locker space, or shed.

- Whatever the setting try to end each day tidying it and creating a 'to do' list for the next day.
- Keep drawers tidy and store similar items together. For example, in an office setting keep stationery in one place, like a pot or a drawer. Label things to remember where they have been kept.
- Try to be consistent about where things are stored, putting them back in the same place every time e.g. tools you use regularly for a job such as a hole punch or stapler, so that you are not wasting time hunting for them. If you wear a jacket or coat to work in then always place specific things in one pocket e.g. keys.
- Use labelled or colour-coded filing trays for different information or different types of tools (for example, use different trays to prioritise your workload). Using different coloured boxes to store items can make it easier to know where they are. Matching tools to task by colour-banding them (wrapping a piece of coloured tape around the handle of the tool) can be helpful.

- If you work on a computer the same principles apply! Keep work tidy by ensuring that there are folders for each task type or theme and work is placed in the folders. If this is hard to do then ask for assistance setting it up.
- Set aside time each week, such as on Friday afternoon, for half an hour, to have a tidy up of notes and papers and create a plan for the following week.
- If you don't work in an office but drive around in a car or van, for example, make sure it doesn't become a dumping ground for empty bottles, crisp packets etc. Have a plastic bag which you can throw rubbish in. Have a comb or brush in the car to tidy up before going into a customer or work. Having an 'emergency kit' in the car can be useful e.g. spare key, phone charger, bottle of water, spare pair of tights (if female) if you tend to forget or lose things quite often.
- If you you lose your passwords and codes then try to use an app that allows you to keep all your passwords in one encrypted database, protected by one password.

  ○ e.g. Universal Password Manager
  ○ *http://upm.sourceforge.net/*

Managing your time at work

Some jobs are naturally very structured and others are not. Whatever type of job it is, it is always possible to plan and schedule time and set priorities. Scheduling and planning are essential to managing workload.

Below are some tips to help manage time at work:

- **Allow additional time for items on the work schedule.** We all think things will take us less time than they actually do. Be realistic and build in extra time in the schedule for interruptions and delays in work.
- **Make and update plans regularly.** Make use of a monthly calendar, a weekly calendar, a day planner, electronic planners and to-do lists/checklists. You can have reminders set for all meetings and appointments by entering them into your mobile phone calendar or your email calendar (e.g. Microsoft Outlook).
- **Try to enter appointments, details, contact person in your diary immediately** they are given. Having information in one place means you can see all the details together rather than hunting all over the place if away from the desk or place of work.
- **Make a <u>short</u> 'to-do' list <u>every</u> day.** Take five minutes at the start or end of each day to make a plan of the jobs/tasks to be completed. Restrict the number of items so it remains realistic (5 or 6). To create your own free online checklist, go to *www.checklist.com* or use an app on your phone:

- ○ **Sorted – The Daily Organiser.**
  *https://itunes.apple.com/gb/app/
  sorted-the-daily-
  organiser/id513269408?mt=8&ign-
  mpt=uo%3D2*
- ○ **24me** *https://itunes.apple.com/PK/app/
  id557745942?mt=8&ign-mpt=uo%3D4*

- **Keep regular plans.** Make plans daily, weekly and monthly; don't wait until work piles up and then there are increasing problems and you cannot meet deadlines. Develop a system, if you can, to make sure that you do certain tasks each week; keeping regular routines makes tasks easier to remember so that they become a habit.
- **Try to prioritise tasks.** Consider when they need to get finished and what can wait. If you are unsure where the priorities are in your work ask your manager/supervisor for guidance.
- **Use technology**, where appropriate. Simple tools built into your phone, for example, can provide alarms to be reminded of deadlines and appointments e.g. *http://www.focusboosterapp.com*. This is an app that breaks down tasks into chunks to assist with focusing.
- Use Post-it notes and attach them in prominent places in order to prompt an action or job that needs to be completed that day. There are also Post-it notes or Stickies that you can download and use on your computer or laptop.

- ○ *www.post-it.com*
- ○ *www.zhornsoftware.co.uk/stickies/index.html*

- Use a notepad, pocket PC or mobile phone to remind you of what you need to do. Even a small notepad in your pocket is useful.
- Use your mobile phone to record things that are easily forgotten or that you might forget to do or create reminders on your mobile phone – take pictures with your phone if that helps you.

  - ○ You could use an app such as Evernote or Dropbox to store them all in one place
  - ○ *https://evernote.com/*
  - ○ *https://www.dropbox.com/*

- Try different ways of note taking:

  - ○ An example of free mind mapping software
  - ○ *http://mind42.com/*

Job coaching

Coaching has been used successfully, particularly for adults with Attention Deficit Hyperactivity Disorder, to help enhance the ability to manage life, day-to-day decisions and set and achieve goals. It usually involves a series of sessions, face-to-face, online or on the phone to develop strategies that work, and take action towards reaching goals. This can help with reflecting on what has worked or not and why.

   This site has some good ideas about what to look for in a coach.

http://aadduk.org/help-support/coaches/

CHAPTER 8

Using technology to assist

Adapting the computer

Changing the colour background on your computer

In Microsoft Office and Apple programs you can change the colour background on all documents without affecting the printing.

Changing the colour background to a cream or other colour may make the screen and text clearer to read.

You can also use magnifying settings to increase the size of the font or to magnify specific text – look at the accessibility options in the Settings.

Screen ruler

A **'Screen ruler'** program is a tool for assisting with reading on the PC and Mac. It provides a strip or ruler across the screen which can have the contrast changed and have the background coloured or greyed out. This is available from:

*http://www.clarosoftware.com/
index.php?cPath=348*

Fonts

Some fonts with 'ticks' and 'tails' at the end of most strokes tend to obscure the shapes of letters, so fonts such as Arial or Verdana are generally easier to read. Increasing the size or spacing of the text can also help readability.

There are a number of other fonts but some need to be purchased.

- Read Regular *www.readregular.com*
- sylexiad (*http://www.robsfonts.com/ sylexiadserif.html*)
- Lexia font which also claims to be Dyslexia-friendly (*http://www.k-type.com/ fontlexia.html*)

Text-to-Speech software (TTS)

TTS software is more and more built in as standard for new computer word packages e.g. Microsoft Office 2010 and Apple both have accessible packages with free TTS – they have a choice of voices and also allow you to speed up or slow down the pace of the words being spoken.

With text-to-speech software the person can hear what is written as well as read the text. There are a variety of programs some of which are free and some you can try out with a trial version before buying.

e.g.

- Balabolka
  - *http://www.cross-plus-a.com/balabolka.htm*

- Announcify for Chrome – you can listen to anything on the web
  - *https://chrome.google.com/webstore/detail/announcify/mmiolkcfamcbpoandjpnefiegkcpeoan*

- Select and speak
  - *https://chrome.google.com/webstore/detail/select-and-speak/gfjopfpjmkcfgjpogepmdjmcnihfpokn*

- Free text-to-speech – some of these listed sell versions with high quality voices:
  - Natural Reader *www.naturalreader.com*
  - Readpal *http://www.readpal.com/one/screenreader.htm*
  - Powertalk – speaks Power Point slides *http://fullmeasure.co.uk/powertalk/*

Speech-to-Text software (STT)

These are programs which allow you to speak into the computer and it types out what you say automatically. These do require some training (only about 15 minutes) and practice to use successfully. A quiet room is also an advantage. Even when the content is typed it is very important to proofread your work as the computer may not have fully understood what you wanted to say.

- Programs available include **'Dragon Naturally Speaking'** and **'IBM Via Voice'** available from *www.microlinkpc.com*
- There are free, more basic versions of these software packages that can be tried for iPAD and iPhone.On iPhone six and beyond there is Siri built in and in Google there is also Voice Search.

Proofreading software

This is able to pick up spelling and grammar errors, and words that sound similar but may mean something different e.g. 'pore' and 'pour'. It can also improve word choices by making alternative suggestions:

- *www.ghotit.com*
- *www.gingersoftware.com*
- *http://www.grammarly.com/*

Touch typing software

Learning to touch type can be an extremely useful skill particularly when completing long assignments. There are a number of web-based programs which teach touch typing skills including:

- *www.bbc.co.uk/typing*
- *www.typingweb.com*
- *www.nimblefingers.com*
- *www.typefastertypingtutor.com/index.html*
- *http://www.learntyping.org/typinggames.htm*

Examples of some commercial packages available:

- Typing Instructor Deluxe
- Ultrakey
- Mavis Beacon Teaches Typing

Apps for typing skills
Some free apps can be downloaded:

Taptyping
  ○ *http://ipad.appstorm.net/how-to/utilities/how-to-improve-your-typing-skills-with-taptyping/*
Typing web
  ○ *http://www.typingweb.com/*
Typing test
  ○ *http://www.typingtest.com/*

Predictive text
Predictive text programs anticipate words and offer suggestions as you type. They also learn words that are used often. They are standard on most phones (although they can be turned off) and help with spelling as well as speed.

Predictive text software can also be used on the desktop or laptop to help get thoughts down quickly.

Let Me Type
Once this gets used to your style this free
　　software offers suggestions as you type.
　　　◦ *www.clasohm.com/lmt/en/*

Typing efficiently

- Shortcuts

Another way to add to keyboard skills is to use
some of the keyboard shortcuts or keystrokes.
Learning a few can really speed up actions.

　http://support.microsoft.com/kb/126449
　http://www.autohotkey.com/board/topic/
　　1738-comprehensive-list-of-windows-hotkeys/

- Auto Hot Key

If you are technically minded, setting up a chain of
operations from one command can save time and
effort.

　http://www.autohotkey.com

Backing up or saving work

- If documents or any work is created on a
  computer then having a system for backing it
  up is essential. Regularly synchronising the
  phone with the computer is a must for updating
  and being able to access information from any
  computer.

- **Memory stick –** this is portable but can also be easily lost. Putting it on a key ring can make it harder to lose.
- **External hard drive –** this can be used to back up every time work has been completed. However you may need to check that this is allowed in your place of work as many employers will have guidelines on information being saved and the method to do so.
- As well as the usual communication tools like SMS, phone and email, there are a number of methods to store ALL files. These allow sharing of files (where allowed) by different work colleagues as well.
- **Web Storage:** allows you to use cloud storage and share information with one or more people through your web browser.

Google Docs

- *https://drive.google.com/?pli=1#my-drive*

Dropbox

- *https://www.dropbox.com*

Check with the employer what the guidelines are for storing and backing up work. Some work settings do not allow the use of USB or hard drives and have an intranet or the Cloud for backup.

Different ways to capture information

Using Excel
Use Excel to create lists with sections, timelines and notes, add colour, use a different workbook for each project. Label each page for easy access:

http://www.youtube.com/watch?v=6IAhk5xZf5A

Diagrams
Use 'Word' Smart-Art to create diagrams with many levels of branches:

http://www.youtube.com/watch?v=AiYPVY55uag

Mind Maps
Mind mapping (also known as brainstorming, spider mapping) software can be used to make detailed plans with many sub-branches:

http://spyrestudios.com/15-great-mindmapping-tools-and-apps/

To make a mind map online the following websites are useful; many of them are free or allow a free trial before buying:

http://www.inspiration.com/WebspirationClassroom
http://www.visual-mind.com/index.php
http://www.visual-mind.com/index.php
http://cayra.en.softonic.com/
http://www.mindmeister.com/mobile

http://www.xmind.net/
http://www.thinkbuzan.com/intl/products/
  imindmap

Sticky Notes
These are like notes you can move around the screen and act as reminders. They usually sit on the desktop of the computer.
  These are already built into Apple and Microsoft programs but can also be downloaded:

http://evernote-sticky-notes.en.softonic.com

Applications (apps) to help with organisation

iPhone apps
There are many applications available on iPhone that can help with organisational skills. Some of the most helpful ones for individuals are listed below.

Maps and compass: mapping out how to get from A to B (e.g. from home to a meeting) is important socially and for work.

- **Google maps:** With Google maps you can pinpoint your location on a map so you can plan journeys or find a building. And when you arrive, you can drop a pin to mark your location and share it with others via email or MMS.
- **Find your car:** these applications help you to find out where your car is parked:

https://play.google.com/store/apps/details?id=
  com.elibera.android.findmycar&hl=en
http://appadvice.com/appguides/show/
  car-finding

- **iPhone car parking application:** This is
  anotherapplication to help you to remember
  where you parked.

  http://appadvice.com/appguides/show/
    car-finding

Android apps

- **Astrid task/'to-do' list:** this app encourages
  and nags you into staying organised. Features
  tagging, reminders, Remember-the-Milk sync,
  adding to calendar, and more!

  https://play.google.com/store/apps/
    details?id=com.timsu.astrid&hl=en
  http://www.rememberthemilk.com/
  Any.Do to do list
  https://play.google.com/store/apps/
    details?id=com.anydo&hl=en

- **Dropbox:** lets you sync and store your files 'in
  the cloud' and access them from another
  Internet-connected device or PC.

  https://www.dropbox.com

- **Evernote:** an easy-to-use, free app that helps you remember everything across all of the devices you use. It lets you take notes, capture photos, create to-do lists, record voice reminders and makes these notes completely searchable, whether you are at home, at work, or out and about.

  https://evernote.com/

- **Diaro:** a personal diary or journal application. You can note down thoughts, experiences and insights. You can attach any number of images to each entry, making this a good tool to also capture key moments in a day.

  http://www.diaroapp.com/

- **Note pads:** allow you to write anything you want e.g. shopping list etc. Set a quick reminder for your note or share it with others by SMS or email.

  https://play.google.com/store/apps/details?id= com.threebanana.notes

- **Calculator:** most phones have in built calculators but there are some others you can download.

  https://play.google.com/store/apps/details?id =org.mmin.handycalc&hl=en

Scientific calculator

> *https://play.google.com/store/apps/details?id
> =com.scientificCalculator&hl=en*

Math calculator

> *https://itunes.apple.com/us/app/mathstudio/
> id439121011*

CHAPTER 9

Getting organised at home

This chapter has some useful hints and tips for helping to get and stay organised in day-to-day life. Individuals with ADHD, Dyspraxia, ASD and Dyslexia often have challenges with their time management and organisational skills.

Estimating how long a task will take to do, planning ahead, sorting possessions so they will be easily found can all be a day-to-day challenge. Disorganisation can result in 'lost' time looking for keys or finding papers, for example, and can increase anxiety levels. Forgetting to do tasks can impact on working function e.g. not washing shirts, and thinking there is another one in the cupboard, but finding you need one to go to work and they are all in a crumpled mess on the floor!

The more tasks that can be automated i.e. doing things at the same time and putting things in the same place, the less effort it takes to remember what to do e.g. always placing keys in the same place when you come into the house or flat means you are not running around the house spending time searching in the morning before going to work.

There is a balance between trying to be ordered and being obsessional about it. Order and consistency help to predict what may happen next. However, dealing with change is important too. In individuals with ASD, variability and change may cause feelings of increased anxiety.

Plan ahead

- **Set aside 20–30 minutes at the end of every day to plan for the next day.** Think about what will be happening today, this week, this month. Having a 'what next' and 'what if' approach helps to plan.
  - What next? – what do you need to have with you for a successful day e.g. specific papers, keys, a USB, phone, money, lunch . . .
  - What if? – think about this as well e.g. what if it rains on the way to work, do you have an umbrella; what if you need to stay late for work, who will feed the dog (if you have one!)?

- **Lay out clothes** for the next day, including shoes etc. Are the shoes clean? Could they be cleaned this evening?
- **Make lunch** for the next day and keep it in the fridge. This will save money and is likely to be healthier than picking something up on the go. Consider putting a Post-it note on the front door as a reminder not to leave without it the next day!

- **Pack a bag** for work/activities the night before ensuring that everything is there e.g. purse/wallet, phone, keys and any important documents.
- **Set an alarm** (or two if heavy sleeping is a problem!) to help get up at the same time every day. Big swings in sleep pattern aren't always helpful as well as making you feel groggy. Use your mobile phone, alarm clock or laptop. Some apps for this:
- *http://www.androidcentral.com/best-alarm-clock-apps-android*
- *http://techpp.com/2013/03/28/alarm-clock-apps-ios-android/*
- **Have something with you to give you the time e.g. phone or watch.** Setting alarms as a pre-warning to do a task can be the greatest assistance with being on time.
- **Make the most of your mobile phone!** Enter all your meetings (e.g. with the bank), appointments (e.g. with your doctor) and social events (e.g. going out for a meal for a friend's birthday) into the calendar function on it. Some phones will sync events from social networking sites such as Facebook with the phone's calendar and will automatically update the calendar with friends' birthdays etc.

Use your time wisely by:

- Using the time of day when you concentrate best for the most demanding work.

- Utilise small blocks of time for 'busy' but not deeply intellectual tasks such as photocopying or sorting out notes.
- Reassess your schedule from time to time. Check that you are keeping up-to-date in all areas. Ask yourself if you need to allocate more time to work generally, or for certain areas, or if you would be more effective working at different times of day/evening.
- Use 'spare' bits of time wisely. For example, a ten-minute bus journey could allow you read an article or write a to-do list to prepare yourself for the day. You could listen on your phone/Kindle/iPAD/notepad to a recording or watch a video.

Routine helps

- Using timetables or schedules can help you to make the most of your time; they can be especially useful for making sure you get all your tasks and chores done and ensuring a home life/work life balance.
- Make a weekly timetable. Try to set aside the same time each week to sit down and make a timetable for the week; even though it feels like a chore it is well worth it! When writing up your timetable try and schedule the same time each week to do certain tasks, like doing your food shopping every Sunday afternoon or your cleaning on a Wednesday evening so that they become routine, and a habit.

- Putting your keys in the same place. Have a dish or hook to place them on every time you come home.

To-do lists

- Make a 'to-do' list – make a list of the things needing to be done (e.g. clean the car, post a letter) and tick it off as completed. DON'T make the list too long – no more than ten items or it becomes too long to complete.
- To create your own free online checklist, go to www.checklist.com.
- A small notepad can be useful but may get lost. Using a mobile phone and backing this up to the computer means information is less likely to get lost.
- Once you have a 'to-do' list for the week you can prioritise your tasks by making a 'to-do' list for each day. You need to prioritise by considering which tasks need to get finished and which can wait.
- Use Post-it notes and attach them in prominent places in order to prompt an action or job that needs to be completed that day. There are even Post-it notes that you can download and use on your computer or laptop, to find out more, go to: www.post-it.com.
- Put your list somewhere you can see it. Having a pin board or magnetic notice board on a wall in your house is really useful! You can pin up important notices and documents for easy

access. For example, the local council's rubbish collection specifications to help you remember what rubbish goes in what bag.

Keeping track of post

- Keep two trays for post and deal with it as it comes in. Place all incoming mail in one tray and open it as it comes through; have a bin by the post and straight away put the junk into it rather than letting it grow.
- Have a box file for all bills so they are kept together and sit down once a month (e.g first Saturday of the month) to go through bills. If you are uncertain how to do this and how to create a plan then ask a friend or family member for assistance.
- Use labelled or colour-coded filing trays for storing information to read, notes to be sorted and bills to be paid.
- Set up Direct Debits for key bills e.g. electricity and water, so the number of incoming bills is reduced, and also the risk of forgetting to pay one.

Lost keys

- Get more than one key cut! It's a good idea to have a spare key with a friend or hidden away somewhere safe.
- Don't ever keep keys close to anything with your address on it, like a key ring, because it could lead to a break-in.

- If keys are lost often, a whistling key finder can help find lost keys.
- A wall keyholder can be mounted outside a flat or housefor keeping keys in. You need a pin code to open it.

> *http://www.easylocks.co.uk/ezlok-magnetic-key-box-safe-disguised-safes-p-3400. html?gclid=CP_OnO6GpLYCFYKN3god5HIAcg*

Planning for shopping and cooking

Being able to cook is a useful part of living independently and will benefit not only health but also the bank balance! Eating the same food all the time may be preferred by some, but may not provide a balanced diet.

Recipes

Keep things simple to begin with. Learn a few key dishes that can be made in one pot or in the microwave (to cut down on washing up!). It can be cost and time effective to make a big pot of something (e.g. a chilli con carne) and freeze portions for another day.

See *www.bbcgoodfood.com* for some useful recipes. Ingredients can be typed in and then the site gives suggestions for recipes.

See *www.visualrecipes.com* for useful visual guides and instructions for a wide array of recipes.

Useful equipment to assist with food preparation

There are many pieces of equipment that can make life easier in regards to cooking, especially if co-ordination is an issue.

For example:

Help with food preparation: chopping boards that have a slip-resistant base.

Help with weighing and measuring: scales with large digital displays, tactile markings and speech output.

Help with peeling, mashing and grating: table-top peelers, handheld utensils with enhanced grip to aid peeling/grating etc.

Help with cooking: cooker adaptations, timers, food thermometers or microwaves with large display or speech output.

Help with eating and drinking: items with advanced grip, battery-operated dispensers, protective clothing.

For more ideas and details on where to buy these items visit *www.livingmadeeasy.org.uk*.

Meal planning

Planning meals will save both time and money.

When planning a meal consider:

- What is going to be made?
- What are the ingredients needed to make the dish?
- What cooking utensils are going to be needed in order to prepare/cook your food?
- Approximately how long is it going to take to make the meal?

For more ideas and help with meal planning and shopping visit:

www.sainsburysdiets.co.uk/OurMealPlans/
   Home?utm_source=google&utm_medium=ppc
http://realfood.tesco.com/meal-planner.html

Food shopping tips to save time and money
Being a careful supermarket shopper is a life skill. Planning meals for each week can save money and increase the chances of eating healthily rather than grabbing a snack because of lack of time.

- Ensure you have some cupboard and freezer staples (e.g. dried pasta, flour, tins of tomatoes etc. to be able to make a quick meal).
- Make a shopping list of things needed every week. These are the staples in your basket e.g. milk, cereal, fruit, yoghurt, toilet paper. Have an additional list for things bought from time to time e.g. washing powder, toilet cleaner, and ketchup.
- Photocopy the list, or have it saved on the phone as a reminder.

- Splitting packs of food and freezing portions can save money (e.g. buying a packet of four chicken breasts, using one and then making three more packs for the freezer).
- Don't go to the supermarket without a list. It's easier to make quick and sometimes expensive decisions if there is no plan. Design a menu for the week and buy according to this.
- Some people find having a two-week cycle of meals can help with budgeting and planning.

Technology to help with food shopping
Consider food shopping online. Most supermarkets offer this and it may be easier than going by bus or on foot. It also minimises the risk of impulse buying.

Before going shopping it is possible to compare supermarket prices to find the cheapest:

www.mysupermarket.co.uk

On iPhones, a 'barcode reader application' can be downloaded allowing items to be added to an 'online' basket when you're on the go. For an example on how to use this application:

www.tesco.com/apps/iphone

Useful websites to help with home organisation, and food preparation

These tools and resources can help you to be more organised at home and with daily living:

Betterware has home storage ideas and for recycling and outdoor garden equipment:

http://www.betterware.co.uk/

Lakeland has many easy-to-use storage solutions:

http://www.lakeland.co.uk/Homepage.action

Planning travel

Most jobs require some travel even if it is from home to work and back again. Plan ahead if you can, so you are fully prepared and become familiar with the journey.

Some jobs require you to go and visit customers, go to meetings or attend training etc. If this is a new journey then try to make sure that is planned in advance.

Consider:

- What's the address?
- What are the travel options e.g. foot, car, train, bus?
- What time do you need leave and return?
- Do you need to book a ticket in advance (often much cheaper)?
- When is it cheaper to travel (off-peak times)?
- If using a bus, train or plane how will you get there from home?
- Do you need to make sure you have some cash on you, as you may be in a hurry?

- Have you left enough time if there is a little delay?
- Print out directions/instructions for the desired location.
- It is a good idea to have a bit of loose change hidden somewhere in the car or on your person to pay for parking or toll bridges etc. as not all take credit cards.
- If there is travel to a lot of new destinations in unfamiliar areas it may be worth investing in a satellite navigation (sat nav) device for your car or buy the download version for the phone.
- Use *www.maps.google.co.uk* to see how far away you are from the bus or train station you need to get you to your destination.
- This website allows for planning a whole journey: *www.transportdirect.com*.

Bus and train time tables and information

Trains:

http://www.nationalrail.co.uk/and
http://www.thetrainline.com/

Buses:

http://www.nationalexpress.com/home.aspx and
http://uk.megabus.com/

Travelling by car

Calculate the journey distance and how long it is expected to take by using a website such as *www.theaa.com/route-planner/index.jsp*. Allow extra time to account for traffic or diversions.

Car sharing schemes

Car sharing schemes and clubs can be useful if you do a regular journey and need to go by car.The link to this article gives some useful advice and warnings on how to stay safe doing so.

http://www.which.co.uk/cars/driving/car-hire-and-car-clubs/car-share-schemes/

Some names of some clubs include:

www.citycarclub.co.uk/
https://www.liftshare.com/uk/

Driving with additional learning needs

Learning to drive a car or motorcycle can prove to be difficult for those with Specific Learning Difficulties, in particular for those with ADHD and Developmental Co-ordination Disorder (Dyspraxia). This may become more important to learn if you are living away from regular public transport. If difficulties persist it may also be an indicator to choose a job near good transport links.

Some people with Specific Learning Difficulties can find it harder to learn to drive and as a result they may take longer to pass their test. This can be related to difficulties when learning a number of new skills and trying to co-ordinate them at the same time. For some it can be harder coping with a changing environment and multi-tasking and reacting at speed. Concentrating, judging distance, steering and using both hands and feet at the same time while changing gears can also be extremely challenging! In addition, having to remember the sequence of the steps necessary to successfully carry out required manoeuvres adds to the difficulty. Some adults with DCD/Dyspraxia find parking particularly hard to do.

Choosing a driving instructor

Seek out an instructor who has taught others who have some challenges or disabilities as they may have more patience and have techniques that may help e.g. knowing how to give instructions using specific markers such as 'turn right at the red building'.

The British School of Motoring (BSM) offers special courses that cater for the needs of people with Specific Learning Difficulties.

Applying for your test

When applying for your driving test ask for extra time to complete the theory/written section if you think you need it. Information about concessions on the theory test is available from:

Drive safe, Driving Standards Agency Special Needs Team

https://www.gov.uk/government/organisations/dr iving-standards-agency

There are books, videos and CD ROMs available that you may find useful preparing for your theory/written test. These are also available from the Driving Standards Agency.

Tips to help with driving

- Start by driving off-road, where all manoeuvres can be practised without having any other cars around.
- Some people find it is easier to start learning in an automatic car rather than using a geared car as there is less to think about.
- Consider taking some simulated lessons before starting out on the road.
- AA has interactive activities on their website:

http://www.theaa.com/aattitude/passing-your-tests/interactive-learning-zone/index.jsp

Once the driving test has been passed

- Use the mirrors to help, even have an extra mirror put in.
- Turn off the radio so you have as few distractions as possible.
- Avoid having a car full of other people if you are not familiar with the journey.
- Become confident on specific routes so you know what to expect before varying routes.
- Think about having rear and front sensors installed to warn you if you get too close to other cars etc.

- Mark the right side of the steering wheel with a red sticker and the left with blue for a quick reminder of right and left.
- Plan your journey in advance. Consider using reverse maps so you don't need to turn the map upside down on the way home! Try websites such as: *http://www.mapquest.co.uk/* or *http://www.theaa.com/.* These can print out instructions rather than following a map.
- Put a clip on the dashboard so you can easily get to the map, but pull on to the side of the road if you are lost.
- If you are lost e.g. finding a destination or service station – stop and ask for directions.
- Take frequent breaks from driving if there is difficulty maintaining concentration.
- Using a sat nav (satellite navigation system) may be distracting rather than a help if you look at the screen and don't keep an eye on the road. Don't 'fiddle' with it when you are driving.
- Phone car parking application. This application can help if you forget where you parked the car. After you find a parking place, just tap 'Park Me!'then when it's time to head back, tap 'Where Did I Park?' and follow the turn-by-turn directions back to the car.

Help and advice with managing money

It is important to budget in order to manage and plan for all outgoings and any unforeseen expenditure. Ignoring this may mean you will end up in a position where debts can mount up and can result in anxiety, and potential loss of a job if money worries impact on work.

Calculate how much your rent and all bills are likely to cost you per month.

For example you may have to pay:

- Rent/mortgage
- Gas
- Electricity
- Water
- Council tax
- Internet connection
- TV license
- Car tax
- Telephone

> *http://www.which.co.uk/money/bills-and-budgeting/guides/how-to-plan-an-effective-budget/five-top-tips-for-balancing-your-budget-/*
> *https://secure.budgettracker.com/login.php?sp=nouser*

Direct debits and standing orders

Where possible organise to pay regular bills with a standing order or direct debit. This is done by completing a form with the bank. It means not having to remember, for example, to pay gas or electricity bills, as the money is taken directly from the bank account.

Many of the banks have specific advice and resources for individuals. Here are some examples:

NatWest

NatWest provides lots of helpful resources to help individuals to manage money Click on the links below to access useful information for the specific areas you may need help with:

*General Advice: http://www.natwest.com/
personal/individuals/g5/individual-
essentials.ashx*

Online banking – Lloyds TSB

Many people manage their funds in their bank by doing this all online. For example, Lloyds TSBClick have made an online demonstration on how to bank online, including paying bills and transferring money. If you think you may like to look at this to gain a general idea of how online banking works then visit the link below:

*http://www.lloydstsb.com/new_internet_banking_
demo/index.html?WT.ac=IBIBD0810*

Barclays

They have a live chat service so you can ask specific questions online if wanted:

*http://www.barclays.co.uk/Helpsupport/
Currentaccountshelpandsupport/
P1242561816563*

iPhone apps

Spending tracker
A free app that is easy to use and tracks spending.

Manilla
This can help with staying on top of bills and consolidate financial accounts under one password. There are automatic reminders to ensure that you don't forget to pay bills and the app offers an organised digital filing cabinet of bills, statements, notices, and offers.

Expensify
This is an app that helps track expenses.

Dealing with unexpected bills

- Don't panic. Can the bill be paid? Is there enough money to pay for it?
- If there is not enough money to pay the bill, discuss with close family what the alternatives are.
- Can some money be borrowed temporarily from them and paid back. If this is done, then make a plan for how the money will be paid back. If you don't you can't ask again!
- Talk to the company to see if you can come to an arrangement where you pay the bill over an extended period of time. Companies are usually quite willing to help if you communicate with them as soon as you recognise you might be in some difficulty.

For more help, advice and tips on managing your money visit the following websites:

Citizens Advice Bureau

http://www.citizensadvice.org.uk/
http://www.debtadvicefoundation.org/
  debt-tools/budget-planner?gclid=
  CJzj3qDu_agCFcJP4QodtknjSA
http://www.moneysavingexpert.com/banking/
  Budget-planning

Payday loans

Payday loans are short-term loans for small amounts of money. They are readily available from high street shops and internet sites.

Payday loans can be easy to get BUT interest rates are very high.

This can lead to further debt being rolled over. Be very wary of taking out one of these!!

http://www.adviceguide.org.uk/england/debt_e/
  debt_borrowing_money_e/
  debt_types_of_borrowing_e/debt_loans_e/
  debt_payday_loans_e/pay_day_loans.htm

CHAPTER 10

Looking after yourself

This chapter provides some guidance around personal care and how to think about what is appropriate dress for the work setting. This chapter is mainly for the employee.

Dressing for work

First impressions are often based on what you are wearing and how you look. For some people this may be of little interest and importance. However, understanding some dress code rules can ensure that you meet minimum accepted standards.

If a uniform is not provided, developing a working wardrobe of clothes is helpful. This simply means having an appropriate array of clothes set aside for work. Doing this should also save time when getting ready for work. This is like developing your own uniform.

Starting a new job is a good time to ask the line manager or HR department whether there are any rules about what to wear to work, sometimes referred to as a dress code. As a guide, have a look at what colleagues are wearing. If a uniform is worn keep it all together in a designated space e.g. in the same drawer or section of a wardrobe.

A general starting point is to consider what type of job is being done and how do you want to portray yourself to others? e.g. if you work in an office environment a pair of black, grey or navy trousers or skirt, a shirt or top with a collar and a pair of smart black shoes. Alternatively, if working in landscape gardening suitable clothes maybe required for pruning plants and cutting grass. If working on a building site there will be health and safety issues such as having specialised footwear.

For more advice on putting together a work wardrobe:

http://www.wikihow.com/dress-for-work

Women:

http://career-advice.monster.co.uk/in-the-workplace/workplace-issues/creating-a-work-wardrobe-for-women/article.aspx

Men:

http://career-advice.monster.co.uk/in-the-workplace/workplace-issues/creating-a-work-wardrobe-for-men/article.aspx

General ideas for work clothes

- Match clothes to the event/activities – ask if uncertain. Is the occasion formal or informal? Some workplaces have 'dress down days' where jeans can be worn, but this may not mean shorts or exposing skin. If you are told 'business casual', ask what this means as it may differ in different settings.

- Look around your work setting and see what others are wearing.
- Keep things simple. It is usually best to avoid wearing more than two additional colours with 'background' ones such as black, beige or white which are neutral tones.
- Look for non-iron, easy fold fabrics so clothes are not crumpled.
- If wearing socks, it's easier not to have lots of different colour socks. Have all the same colour or two different colours of socks, so if you lose one you should still be able to find a pair.
- If going out socially ask what people will be wearing – e.g. going bowling may be jeans and trainers; going to a work-do, may be a dress or smart trousers and a shirt.

Looking after clothes

- When washing clothes hang them up while wet. This reduces the need to iron.
- Change clothes regularly. Smelly is never a great idea!
- Storing trousers and shirts on clothes hangers and hanging them up helps keep clothes crease-free.
- Try using separate baskets or drawers for storing underwear and socks.

- If there is a difficulty with new fastenings/buttons, practise them when you are not wearing the clothes.
- Patterned fabrics mask stains/marks better than plain ones.
- Buy clothes with few or no fastenings such as trousers with easy fastenings.
- If you have weaker co-ordination when dressing/undressing, make sure you are in a balanced position. Dressing while sat on the floor may make the task easier.

Looking after personal care

Some people find aspects of personal care and dressing challenging e.g. individuals with Dyspraxia/DCD may find specific tasks harder to do because of co-ordination difficulties such as ironing a shirt or folding them neatly. For others it may be confusing working out what the dress code is and how to dress for different settings. It is extremely important to be clean and tidy for work. Your personal hygiene is something your employer and colleagues will be conscious of and they may make judgements based on how well you present yourself at work. Bad personal hygiene is generally not tolerated in society.

For further tips on grooming and personal hygiene visit:

*http://career-advice.monster.co.uk/job-
     interview/preparing-for-job-interviews/how-to-
     groom-yourself-for-a-job-interview-video-
     advice/article.aspx*

Teeth

- An electric toothbrush may be easier and help you to be more thorough.
- Have teeth regularly checked and cleaned by a dentist or hygienist.
- Use an anti-bacterial mouthwash.
- For fresh smelling breath when out keep some sugar-free chewing gum or mints with you.
- Bad breath is never great for making friends!

Shaving/hair removal

- Electric shavers can be easier to use than a hand shaver.
- Choose a shaver that has a built-in safety guard.
- Use shaving foam, as you can see where you have shaved.
- A good magnifying mirror will make it easier to remove facial hair.
- If this is a big problem, consider having laser hair removal which is permanent.

Bathing/showering/toileting

- Using toilet wipes after using the toilet can be more effective than standard toilet paper.
- If balance is poor consider having a seat fitted in the shower. Having a strong handrail fitted by the bath/shower may also be useful.
- A bath mat placed in the bath/shower reduces the risk of falling.
- A long-handled sponge will help wash areas of the body which may be harder to reach.
- If turning taps on/off is hard try long-handled tap turners.
- If showering is difficult use shower crème etc. in the bath and have a soak.
- Put on a towelling robe after a shower. This can be easier than using a towel.
- Remember to tidy the bathroom after finishing using it, especially if living with others i.e. fold the towel, and put the bath mat over the bath or on the radiator, pick up any clothes and take them to the bedroom.

Eating and drinking

If co-ordination is harder:

- Try not to over fill cups with too much liquid.
- Using cups with larger handles provides a better grip.
- A kettle tipper may help make pouring easier and safer.

- Use non-stick matting or a damp dishcloth under plates to stop them moving.
- Use an electronic can opener.
- Sit down to eat when possible – it's usually less messy.

Make-up

- A make-up lesson is a useful way of finding out what colours and styles suit you and easy ways to apply make-up. Go to a large department store – they may offer this free.
- Some make-up can be easier to use than others e.g. tinted moisturisers as an alternative to foundation, lip glosses as an alternative to lipstick and crème eye-shadow which can be applied with fingers instead of powder which usually requires a brush application.
- If mascara is hard to put on, then think about having eyelashes dyed. This only needs to be done a few times a year and will save on time and daily smudging mistakes.
- Sit down to put on make-up, especially if there are difficulties with fine motor control.
- Putting make-up on in a set order will help it become a routine and habit. This will also help reduce mistakes.
- Using a good magnifying mirror can make it easier to see what you are trying to achieve.
- Restrict the number of colours for eye shadow and lipstick. This makes it easier to get it right. Stick to colours that complement your skin tone

and eye colour rather than the colour of the clothes. It is also important to remove make-up thoroughly at the end of the day. Facial wipes rather than cleansers and cotton wool can save time.

- Ask a friend for honest feedback on what the make-up looks like.

Hair

- Having a haircut that is easy to style can save time and effort i.e. needing little blow drying and styling. There are many different styling products available now that make styling hair easier to do.
- Look for blow-dry sprays and straightening lotions to save styling time.
- Using a long-handled hairbrush and/or comb can help reach and look after the back of the hair.
- Longer hair can be tied up or held back using a hair clip.

Eyebrows

- A local beautician or hairdressing salon may offer to shape eyebrows if this is harder to do accurately. There are different options such as plucking, waxing or threading.
- A small magnifying mirror will make it easier to see what is being done and good quality tweezers are better than cheap ones.

Shaving/hair removal

- Shaving legs may be easier if standing or sitting on the edge of the bath if balancing is hard to do.
- Consider visiting a salon/spa for regular waxing to limit the amount of hair removal that needs to be done week to week. Another option is to have laser treatment to permanently remove hair.

CHAPTER 11

Socialising with others in work and out of work

Starting a job is a new and exciting experience, but the thought of not knowing anybody can be a daunting prospect. This chapter is designed to prepare for the social side of work and home life by giving some tips and advice on what is appropriate and what is not in differing settings.

If school was challenging and making and keeping friends was hard to do, confidence may be at a low ebb. A new job can be a new chance to leave any negative experiences in the past and 're-invent' yourself. You can be who you want to be. However, this does not mean making up a 'fantasy' version and lying about your persona. It is important to recognise that you don't need to tell everyone everything about yourself in great detail. Waiting for others to talk about themselves is a useful rule. If there are specific challenges e.g. with literacy or communication skills, do consider telling the employer how they present and what strategies or adjustments can be made.

Telling the difference between work friends, acquaintances, and close friends

A work friend

You need to make sure you don't assume someone is a friend because they are friendly with you. An unbalanced relationship with you being over assertive or too friendly can make others uncomfortable. Watch for signs they want to do something socially, or offer to meet for a coffee. If they don't want to, be friendly but not too 'pushy'.

An acquaintance

This is someone you have recently only met or you have not engaged in conversation or communication. They are not a close friend, so try to avoid giving personal details about yourself, and don't ask personal questions about them. Talk about things you have in common, such as work, to start with. Other safe topics may be about going on holiday and the weather.

A best or close friend

Someone you have usually known for some time. You may have known them since college or school days or be a family friend. You may not see them that often but you always get on well with them and they seem to understand you.

Getting to know someone and making friends

Recognising the signs of someone wanting to be friendly with you:

- They may initiate a conversation with you
- They ask about you and your personal life. e.g.'how was your weekend?'
- Do they make any plans to meet up with you out of work, or ask you to go and have lunch or a coffee/tea with you?
- What are they like if you feel upset? Do they seem to care or ask you how you are?

Signs that someone may not be your friend:

- If they seem to only want to be friendly when you have something to offer them e.g. lending them money, borrowing something from you, if you are having a party, then these may be signs you could be being used or taken advantage of
- Not asking about you and how you are at all
- Not asking you out to anything socially or including you with other colleagues in an activity, discussion they are leading on
- Making rude or cruel comments about you as if it was funny
- Avoiding being with you.

Social skills and confidence building

Work is often a way to make friends, but it may not be possible if you work in a small work environment such as an office setting with only two or three people who may be a different age from you or have different interests.

Below are some ideas to extend your social life. First decide what type of setting you like to be in:

- Do you prefer being with a large or small group of people?
- Do you prefer socialising in the day time or evening?
- Can you travel to an event or place easily or are you limited in how far you can go?
- What are your interests?

  - Are you sporty or do you prefer the arts, opera, listening to bands, helping others, working on the computer, playing games?
  - Do you follow a sport or particular team e.g. football, cricket or tennis?

- Which do you prefer, having background noise or music playing loudly?
- What type of music do you like?

Remember

- You won't improve your social skills and confidence without any practice
- You will make mistakes – everyone does

- You will feel more comfortable making friends if you are in an environment where you have some things in common
- Know what will be expected of you in that environment so you understand the context and the rules of that setting
- Ask others you trust if you are uncertain
- If you have a good friend you can go with ask them to give you some tips
- Try to show you are interested in the person who is talking to you – nod, smile, repeat back phrases to show you have heard, clarify if you are not sure.

Some links and resources that may assist

- *http://appadvice.com/appguides/show/body-language-apps*
- *http://www.autism.org.uk/living-with-autism/communicating-and-interacting/social-skills/social-skills-for-adolescents-and-adults.aspx*
- Growing Up on the Spectrum: A Guide to Life, Love, and Learning for Teens and Young Adults with Autism and Asperger's by Lynn Kern Koegel and Claire La Zebnik

Social and fitness ideas

Some suggestions of fitness and social activities are below. These have been considered as ones that many individuals with Specific Learning Difficulties have reported that they have enjoyed. This is not a limited list. Any hobby can be tried.

- Archery
- Bowling
- Canoeing
- Computer games
- Debating society
- Environmental clubs
- Martial arts
- Music society
- Rambling club
- Rowing
- Salsa dancing
- Sports/Gym clubs
- Volunteering
- Yoga

Meeting others

First think about the following:

- Do you prefer to be one to one, small group or big group?
- A quiet or noisy environment?
- Indoor our outdoors?
- Familiar settings or somewhere new?
- Trying something daring or being cautious?
- Talking or doing?
- Being an observer e.g. watching sport or listening to a band?
- Being a participator e.g. team sport, or in the band or a play, pub team?
- Learning something e.g. an evening class or new sport?

- **Clubs**
  Some people like going clubbing and dancing.
  Others find this a setting they would avoid at all
  costs for several reasons:

  - They are a noisy environment and it may be
    hard to be able to hear any conversation
    happening between you and the other people
  - Dancing may be difficult to do
  - There is a lack of confidence talking with new
    people of same or opposite sex
  - Difficulties tolerating alcohol
  - Difficulties drinking alcohol to excess if/when
    available
  - Making impulsive decisions you regret
    afterwards
  - People too close.

- **Pubs**

  - May be quieter than clubs (but not always)
  - Smaller groups
  - Offer pub quizzes to meet others.

- **Evening classes**
  Find out from your local college or from the
  local library what courses are on – sometimes
  they have one day or short courses that run
  throughout the year.

- **Dating sites and meetings**
  There are numerous online dating agencies and speed dating services – make sure that you check what you are paying for. Always meet someone in a safe place such as a coffee bar or café and let others know where you are and what you are doing. Speed dating can be a good way to practise 'chat up' lines and see what works.

  Some organisations just organise events to meet people e.g. *https://www.citysocializer.com/*

Do remember:

  Look like you have made an effort – clean clothes, clean hair, and clean teeth, and smell good (i.e. use a deodorant).

  Practise some short pieces about yourself that are interesting or have some questions prepared to ask the person you are talking to e.g. 'What's your favourite movie?' 'Where's the place you most want to travel to?' 'If you could be taken out on a date where would the best place for you to go?'

- **Religious groups**
  If you have a specific religion you may find social opportunities to meet others of a similar faith.

- **Sports clubs**
  Tennis clubs and gyms, for example, offer opportunities for meeting others with similar interests. You may want to try out something different such as yoga or karate to meet other people. Some clubs have 'taster' sessions which are often free for you to see what the sport is like before committing to joining.

  http://www.uksportsassociation.org/
  http://hidden-disabilities-in-sport.org/

- **Networking**
  In many towns and cities there will be opportunities to network through business groups or doing volunteering etc.
  http://www.roundtable.co.uk/

- **Volunteering**
  This can be an opportunity to do something quite different to your 'day job' and meet a new group of people. It can also be a way of extending your CV and finding new job opportunities. There are also organisations that can plan a volunteering place abroad for a period of time.

  http://www.csv.org.uk/?display=volunteering
  http://www.vso.org.uk/volunteer
  http://www.volunteering.org.uk/
  http://www.volunteering-wales.net/
  http://www.volunteerscotland.org.uk/
  http://www.volunteer.ie/

CHAPTER 12

Mental health and well-being

There is research evidence that individuals with Specific Learning Difficulties such as Dyslexia, ADHD, ASD and Dyspraxia have a higher risk of some mental health conditions such as anxiety and depression.

Why someone is at greater risk Is a complex picture. This may be related to the fact that if things are harder to do from a younger age it may cause increased anxiety e.g. a child with Dyspraxia who can't throw and catch a ball may become more anxious every time there is PE at school.

A child with Dyslexia who has to read in school may be nervous of doing so which affects their self-confidence and well-being. Adults report these situations and there is also research evidence to back it up. This may also be related to common neurotransmitters in the brain being affected such as Dopamine and Nor Adrenaline in e.g. ADHD, depression and anxiety. Whatever the cause, it still remains important in considering ways to maintain mental well-being.

Mental health is how we think, feel and behave.

What is stress?

Stress is when an individual has a feeling that they are not coping. This can be caused by internal factors such as ill health, and external factors such as bullying in the workplace or not coping with job demands placed on them.

People react to this very differently. Some people can have a physical reaction and have headaches, stomach aches and back pain as a 'marker' of feeling stressed.

Others may have a psychological reaction to stress and may not be able to sleep, or feel anxious or depressed if it continues for some time.

Stress in the workplace can be related to a number of factors:

- Risk of losing a job
- Harassment or bullying
- Lack of work
- Too much work
- Lack of training.

However, not all stress is bad for you. Having an element of stress in one's life may motivate you to get up in the morning and go to work. If you are too 'laid back' you may not feel it is worth doing anything or strive to improve your skills. However, if it all gets too much then it can make you feel out of control and end up in burn out, increased anxiety and depression.

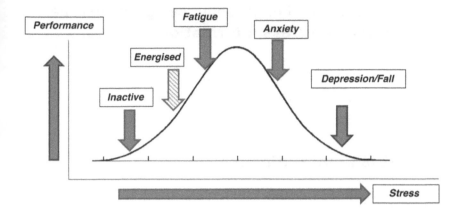

When considering workplace stress it is also important to think of the whole person, as the effect of challenges in home life can impact on work:

- getting married
- having a baby
- moving house
- death
- divorce
- caring for a parent or child
- ill health in you or others
- financial difficulties.

The accumulation of some factors at home and some at work can have a combined effect and act as a 'tipping point' for some people. Understanding the triggers and consequent symptoms, which may be both physical e.g. back ache, stomach pains, headaches, or psychological e.g. poor sleep, feeling low, feeling irritable or angry, is important to

prevent 'burn out' i.e. no longer being able to cope.
Work related stress information

http://www.hse.gov.uk/stress/
http://www.mindfulemployer.net/
   Work-Related%20Stress.pdf

What is mental illness?

Mental illness can impact on your:

- well-being
- performance day to day
- increase your sickness rates
- productivityin the workplace.

Workplace triggers that may increase the risk of mental health conditions

- managing constant changes in work patterns
- bullying or harassment by others
- not having the skills for the job
- unrealistic deadlines
- under-stretched
- fear of loss of job leading to 'presenteeism' (being there but not working at your best)
- home factors affecting sleep and concentration
- physical illness
- relationships with peers or line managers
- others in the team off sick or on leave
- disciplinary or grievance procedures.

You may show signs and symptoms (to others) in a number of ways, including a change in the way you have behaved previously.
These may include:

- being angry with others
- being withdrawn, or appearing very quiet
- being irritable with others
- being tearful
- smoking, drinking, eating more
- acting tired or lacking energy
- lacking interest in work
- missing deadlines
- being late for meetings.

Ways of asking for help from work if you are feeling anxious, depressed or stressed

- Discussing with the line manager about what can help, with examples where possible about what has worked in the past.
- Being specific about what is difficult in work e.g. have there been increased demands without training; change in working hours; new line manager and there is uncertainty about their ways of working; a new skill expected.
- If off ill, then maintaining contact and having an open and honest discussion about return to work will be useful and allowing a Return to Work Plan to be developed together.

- Developing a Staying Well Plan – this allows others to recognise if the individual is becoming ill again.
- Having a discussion between employee and employer about using any paid or unpaid leave for hospital or GP appointments.
- Discussing how leave or holidays can be be planned at set times rather than in bigger blocks.
- Considering the potential for working flexible hours e.g. missing peak travel times, regular hours avoiding shift changes.
- Discussing the possibility of even extending the day and having longer midday breaks to cope with workload and having time to rest.
- Thinking about whether there are home and work issues that have not been addressed and need some help e.g. travel, care and financial issues.

Suggested reasonable adjustments to the job if someone has had a mental illness

- A temporary reduction in the volume of work to gain control and put in place some training or support.
- If the job has changed, then considering if there are training needs and organising training for them.
- Discussing with HR or the line manager, co-workers, about communication or relationship difficulties that need to be addressed.

- Discussing whether deadlines are reasonable and if the individual is being asked to do work beyond their ability and capability. Considering whether a review of the job description needs to be undertaken.
- Ensuring a clear appraisal and review process is in place so there is time to discuss issues.
- Considering whether a buddy or work mentor may be of assistance.
- Discussing the need for an Access to Work assessment for additional support.

Preventing burnout and looking after yourself

Keeping well and coping in a stressful job means making sure that you don't wait until you are too tired or not coping and risk losing your job from poor performance:

- Plan leave and try to take it all.
- Space out leave across the year so there is not a point of complete exhaustion.
- Having a break or holiday booked means something to focus on.
- Create a time for yourself at home, even if it is a ten minute walk in the park, sitting and meditating for ten minutes a day, listening to some favourite music or taking a long soak in the bath.

- Take some regular exercise – exercise improves the quality of sleep and in turn will provide more stamina for work.
- Eat healthily – you are no different from a car – good quality food is needed to function. Avoid excess alcohol especially during the working week that may affect work performance the following day.
- Try to have a regular sleep pattern rather than large swings from day to day e.g. going to bed when tired but getting up the same time. We all need about six to eight hours a night to function fully.
- Avoid excess drinking of alcohol or use of drugs as this can have a short and longer term impact on work, relationships and mental well-being.

Seeking professional help for mental health issues

If feelings of anxiety, depression, low mood have been going on for more than two weeks then talking to the GP may be helpful to gain their view and some assistance.

This is especially true if symptoms include the following:

- difficulties with sleep
- crying for no apparent reason
- feeling very low
- change in eating pattern – eating more or less

- avoiding socialising with others compared to previously
- increasing missed deadlines for work
- early morning waking and worrying excessively.

The GP may offer a talking therapy such as Cognitive Behavioural Therapy or may offer medication as well, where appropriate.

For more information:

> *http://www.rcpsych.ac.uk/expertadvice/*
>   *treatments/cbt.aspx*
> *http://www.mind.org.uk/mental_health_a-z/*
>   *8000_cognitive_behaviour_therapy*

This site also has some great strategies to assist: *http://www.llttf.com*

Reducing risks and improving mental well-being

Alcohol and socialising

Know your limits! Binge and excess drinking on a regular basis can affect your health both in the short and longer term. In particular some people with DCD/Dyspraxia have described that their co-ordination is made worse by drinking and they appear to be more sensitive to the effects. Other people find that because they may be impulsive, they drink before thinking, and then drink to excess, only realising the impact too late in the night (or following morning!). If you have drunk too much, you will be less aware of others behaviour towards you and may not be able to predict soon enough that you could also be at risk.

If you are worried that drinking alcohol is interfering with your daily life then speak to your doctor or use the helpful organisations below for advice:

- *www.drinkaware.co.uk*
- *www.talktofrank.com/drugs.aspx?id=166*
- *www.nhs.uk/livewell/alcohol/pages/ alcoholhome.aspx*

Fitness can help with wellbeing
Being fit helps both physical and mental well-being, and assists in the ability to cope with both home and work life. Just working out regularly for 15 to 20 minutes a few times a week can have a positive effect on motor skills, confidence and well-being.

- Getting started is the hardest step to take. Small changes can make a difference. Integrating activities into everyday occurrences makes this a little easier e.g. walking up stairs rather than using the lift at work; getting off the bus one stop earlier and walking that extra mile; taking ten minutes of your lunch to stretch, walk or do some exercise every other day.
- Try non-competitive sports and evening classes such as swimming, walking, yoga, Tai Kwando and other martial arts.

- Understand that it may take you longer to be confident in learning a new activity or skill.
- Joining an evening or day class to learn or improve a hobby or skill can offer an opportunity for making new friends. It can be an opportunity to meet others with similar interests and allows conversations to be natural and focused on a shared interest. Gaining confidence out of work can also help in work and can provide a topic of conversation.
- There are some tools that can assist you to get fit and track your progress:

  ○ Nike+ SportWatch tracks time, distance, pace, heart rate and even the number of calories you've burned, but you do have to pay for this.
  ○ *http://www.loseit.com/what-is-lose-it/* is an app which sets a daily calorie budget, tracks your food and exercise, and may help you to stay motivated and achieve your goal.

Useful resources and contacts for mental well-being

Counselling
This website shows individuals where to find their nearest individual counselling services:

http://www.individual.counselling.co.uk/

Royal College of Psychiatrists
This site has many resources and free leaflets with guidance for the individual and also employers:

http://www.rcpsych.ac.uk/

Samaritans
Samaritans provides confidential non-judgemental emotional support, 24 hours a day for people who are experiencing feelings of distress or despair by phone, face-to-face, by email or by letter:

http://www.samaritans.org/

Depression Alliance
The following organisation works to relieve and prevent depression:

http://www.depressionalliance.org/

Mind
This is to ensure anyone with a mental health problem has somewhere to turn for advice and support:

http://www.mind.org.uk/

Mindfullness
Useful links to resources:

http://www.mindfulnet.org/

Relaxation apps

*https://itunes.apple.com/au/app/
    smiling-mind/id560442518?ls=1&mt=8*
*https://play.google.com/store/apps/
    details?id=com.makanstudios.conscious*
*https://itunes.apple.com/us/app/
    relaxing-sounds-nature-lite/id345747251*
*https://itunes.apple.com/us/app/
    pocket-pond-2/id498375421*
*https://itunes.apple.com/us/app/
    mindrelax-lite/id412085700*
*https://itunes.apple.com/en/app/
    naturespace-relax-meditate/id312618509*

CHAPTER 13

Employer guidance

The suggestions in this chapter are a guide for employers to becoming more 'disability confident' and to ensure all processes are appropriate and accessible, starting from pre-employment, through to job placement and retention.

Many of the suggestions are good, not only for individuals with Specific Learning Difficulties/hidden impairments, but for all potential and current employees. Most are low or no cost solutions.

Around 10 per cent of the population have Specific Learning Difficulties. It is important to be aware of how these difficulties present and what employers can do to maximise the potential of the workforce and work towards compliance under the Equality Act. This should not be the only motivation to take someone on in employment with a hidden impairment. The individual's strengths and view on the world may also offer advantages in solving and supporting the business or organisation (whatever the setting) in a different way.

The Equality Act 2010

The Equality Act came into force from October 2010 providing a modern, single legal framework with clear, streamlined law to more effectively tackle disadvantage and discrimination. Before this the Disability Discrimination Act was in place.

What do the terms mean?

Discrimination types

Direct discrimination
The less favourable treatment of a person compared with another person because of a protected characteristic.

Indirect discrimination
The use of an apparently neutral practice, provision or criterion which puts people with a particular protected characteristic at a disadvantage compared with others who do not share that characteristic, and applying the practice, provision or criterion cannot be objectively justified.

What's a reasonable adjustment?

Equality Law recognises that bringing about equality for disabled people may mean changing the way in which employment is structured, the removal of physical barriers and/or providing extra support for a disabled worker. This is the duty to make reasonable adjustments.

The duty

- The duty to make reasonable adjustments aims to make sure that, as far as is reasonable, a disabled worker has the **same access to everything that is involved in doing and keeping a job as a non-disabled person**.
- Each disabled person is individual and therefore has an individual set of needs and adjustments.
- Consultation at regular intervals is important as these needs may change over time or in different contexts.

Protected characteristics

These are the grounds upon which discrimination is unlawful:

- Age
- Disability e.g DCD/Dyspraxia /Autism/Dyslexia
- Gender re-assignment
- Marriage and civil partnership
- Pregnancy and maternity
- Race
- Religion and belief
- Gender
- Sexual orientation.

Further guidance

http://www.equalityhumanrights.com/advice-and-guidance/new-equality-act-guidance/equality-act-guidance-downloads/

Helping as an employer

With the right support, individuals with Specific Learning Difficulties can make a valuable contribution to you as an employer.

If an employee discloses a Specific Learning Difficulty to you it is important to be understanding as the decision to disclose their disability to you may have caused them a lot of anxiety, and feelings of uncertainty about how the information will be received. They may also be concerned about what colleagues may think.

Ask your employee how they feel their difficulties affect them in the workplace and where they consider they need some additional support, if any. Every person is different and their pattern of strengths and challenges will vary despite two people having the same diagnosis.

Strategies to support an employee with a specific learning difficulty will vary depending on many factors. Most adjustments can be made without incurring any cost, however, if you find that an employee needs a level of support that may incur costs (e.g. computer software) then employers can apply for funding through the government's Access to Work scheme. As an employer, doing nothing is not an option under the Equality Act, and not knowing is not able to be used as an excuse for not implementing supportive strategies.

The UK government has the Access to Work programme to help employers support individuals with disabilities in work.

For more information: *https://www.gov.uk/ access-to-work*

General information on hidden impairments

It is essential to look for evidence of interest and level of motivation when considering someone for a job, as many individuals with Specific Learning Difficulties will work hard to overcome their challenges in order to be successful.

- Individuals with Specific Learning Difficulties and mental health challenges don't come in a 'neat box' packaged and labelled. Each individual has their own specific pattern of strengths and challenges.
- Many individuals may not have had a formal diagnosis in childhood. Individuals may vary widely from one another despite having a similar diagnosis.
- Each hidden impairment term is an 'umbrella' term with a spectrum of presentation and varying degrees of impact in the workplace.
- Ask what helps, and what is a challenge for the individual.
- Most Specific Learning Difficulties overlap with one another, so someone may have a 'bit of ADHD' and a 'bit of Dyslexia'. Each person is different.

See **Chapter 1** and **Chapter 2** for more detailed information.

Creating policies and practices in your work setting

With the right support and understanding individuals with Specific Learning Difficulties can make a valuable contribution to employers. However, not understanding what the terms mean, and how they may present, can result in some employers being cautious about employing someone with hidden impairments and feeling confident in supporting them.

Specific Learning Difficulties can pose a challenge to some employers in the workplace, as individuals may not have obvious signs of a disability and their challenges may present in different ways depending on the individual, the nature and severity of the specific difficulties and the different demands and aspects of a job.

People with Specific Learning Difficulties such as Dyslexia and ADHD may not consider themselves to have a disability as such. Indeed, some scholars argue that these difficulties in specific areas can lead to strengths in other areas. The 'hidden' nature of these difficulties can lead to issues concerning disclosing them, and thus the consequent provision, or not, of any support. Given the high levels of Specific Learning Difficulties in the population (10–15%) and the levels of overlap between different disorders (e.g. Dyslexia and Dyspraxia overlap around one third of the time), it is advisable to approach every employee individually to understand their pattern of strengths and difficulties.

For example, an individual may disclose that they have received a diagnosis of Dyslexia and therefore need support with reading, writing and note-taking in the workplace. However this individual may also have difficulties with organising their workspace or prioritising their workload which may not necessarily be catered for by addressing their difficulties specifically associated with Dyslexia. Addressing the individual as opposed to their diagnosis of Dyslexia ensures that they get the support they need and makes them a valuable contributor to the workplace.

Being Disability Confident

All employers can become 'disability confident'. In July 2013 the government in the UK launched a two year campaign to encourage this.

- A disability confident organisation is an organisation that puts policies into practice to ensure people with disability are included.
- Managers in a disability confident organisation know it is important to their business to employ people with disability. They have plans to ensure a diverse workplace.
- Managers and staff in a disability confident organisation understand disability. They know what people with disability can do, and have identified ways to address barriers to employment or promotion for people with disability.

Useful links for more information:

*https://www.gov.uk/government/publications/
    the-disability-confident-campaign
http://jobaccess.gov.au/content/
    being-disability-confident-organisation*

Championing best practice

There are several ways companies can champion best practice:

- **Ensure the organisation considers the individual with hidden impairments in all its policies**
  It can help by considering some theoretical case studies relevant to your business and then testing your processes against these. For example, what if a person can't handwrite, or does this very slowly and inaccurately, and has poor fine motor co-ordination?

  - What does this mean when applying for a job?
  - Signing in when they arrive each day?
  - Signing for consignments?
  - Writing reports?
  - Punching in a pin code to enter a building?
  - Pouring drinks?

Take each descriptor in **Chapter 2** and then consider if someone with this condition was in the business with these challenges whether the organisation would know how to encourage them to apply and work there.

- **Consider how you can have workplace champions** who agree to discuss their disabilities and how they have found ways to work and what support they have received. This allows others with and without difficulties to see the potential to do well, and understand that having someone with the condition in the business can bring positive benefits. This also allows other employees to understand more about the conditions and how they affect individuals.
- **Make sure your literature, paper or website highlight how the organisation supports individuals with a range of hidden impairments and specifically mentions the conditions.** Potential employees will look and see whether there is anything on a website where they are making an application and, where available, will search using key words.
- **Don't just focus on and champion Dyslexia.** This is a great start but remember, for example, around three per cent of the population have Dyspraxia as well, and all these conditions overlap with one another. Have case studies on your website with examples of what has been done to help.

- **Ensure all staff has some understanding of hidden impairments** – signposting them to information sources or providing some training.
- **Gain an understanding of the government schemes available to support the employer and employee** e.g. Access to Work (*http://www.dwp.gov.uk/docs/ employer-guide-atw.pdf*)
- **Talk to other employers about what you have achieved and the impact it has had in the organisation.** Good stories can spread and give models of good practice to others.
- Displaying the 'two ticks' symbol: *https://www.gov.uk/recruitment-disabled-people/encouraging-applications*

Setting up procedures

It is important when setting up and creating policies and procedures in any business or organisation to think about ALL stages from recruitment, interview, and induction to retention.

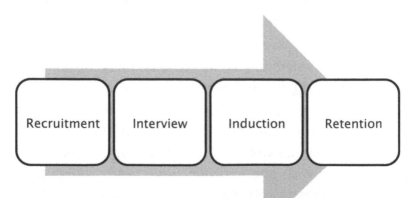

Recruitment   Interview   Induction   Retention

Here are some key pointers for this:

Website and advertisements

- Check that written materials presented are accessible to differing levels of reading ability. Check readability levels. *http://www.read-able.com/*
- Here are a couple of links to discuss how you can make your website accessible:
  http://www.w3.org/WAI/
  http://www.web-accessibility.org.uk/
- Consider the needs of individuals with differing disabilities e.g. ensuring the language used lacks ambiguity; the ability to vary the font choice; Text-to-Speech enabled; limiting text entry or ensuring there is a spell checker being used.
- Ensure that the job application forms and other written materials are in an easy-to-read font such as Arial, Comic Sans Serif – font size 12+ or can be changed to suit the reader. Consider the colour contrast of text on a background that is not a black text on a bright white background.
- Consider how the application process fits in with the actual job. What skills are really required for the job? If this is not IT, then accept telephone interviews and paper applications.
- Check whether there are clear directions and signposting on where to complete job applications or to seek vacancies on the website.

- Show how you support individuals with hidden impairments – are there key search words built into the search engine?
- Check that you have alternative formats for applications on offer for someone with a learning difficulty/disability such as using the phone, or coming in for a discussion.
- Completing online forms – some individuals who have difficulty reading, are slower to understand the information, or have difficulties keying in the information may find it very hard if there is a 'time out' on completion. This can result in them getting half-way through the procedure and then having to start time and time again. This can be disconcerting for them and may put off a potentially excellent applicant.
- Limit free text box completion – if there are free text boxes ensure there is a spell checker on them to assist those with literacy difficulties.
- Consider applying for the Two Ticks symbol if you are in the UK: *https://www.gov.uk/recruitment-disabled-people/encouraging-applications*
- A best practice approach to recruitment advertising would be to include a welcoming and encouraging statement in your advertisements being positive about the people you recruit. See: *http://businessdisabilityforum.org.uk/talent-recruitment*

Applying for jobs online

- Try to avoid requesting handwritten applications or cover notes. Ensure adverts are clearly worded listing only the skills/qualifications that are absolutely essential for the job.
- Consider how the person specification and job description are a true reflection of the job e.g. does a warehouse job really need someone with good communication skills or does someone applying for a job as a shelf stacker need to use the computer? The job description should also be examined and amended so that potential discriminatory criteria are avoided.
- Check how long the application process takes.
- Ensure that the application does not 'time out' half-way through and that the candidate can complete it in if necessary in several sessions.
- Consider whether online applications are always the best format or are you 'ruling out' potential individuals for the job?
- Ensure any web-based application forms are 'stable' and boxes don't move or lose their format when being completed.
- Offer telephone completion of applications as an alternative.
- Check if the application process can be read out on a Text-to-Speech reader.
- Ensure there is somewhere on the form that allows the individual to ask for specific reasonable adjustments for the interview, if required, and information on who to contact to arrange this.

Shortlisting

- Selection criteria must not discriminate against disabled people.
- If telephone interviews are used as a means of selection, someone who has a communication impairment may need to be waived through this process, not to be disadvantaged. If a phone interview is taking place and it is clear there are difficulties for the individual, an alternative should be considered and a suspension of the interview undertaken.
- If this is an online application, does the job require someone to be IT literate? Is this a fair way to decide eligibility for the job? What level of literacy is actually required? If there is a timed element to complete the form, is this a disadvantage to someone who has literacy challenges?
- When you know that the applicant has a hidden impairment:

  - You must take account of how reasonable adjustments could enable the individual to meet the requirements of the person specification.
  - Assess whether or not the person meets, or would meet, your criteria with these reasonable adjustments in place.
  - Be flexible when thinking about how these criteria can be met by a disabled person – the question is can they be met, not how.

Pre-interview

General approaches

- All interviews should be conducted in a fair and consistent manner.
- The applicant should be given details in advance of how the selection process will run.
- Have you considered the tasks you are asking someone to do and thought about whether they are fit for the job i.e. measuring the skills you require or would expect after they have been inducted into the job. If 'excellent communication' is stated on the job description, is it really necessary or will 'good' do?
- Consider the setting where the interview is taking place i.e. is it noisy or distractible e.g. a window into an open plan office?
- Is there somewhere where the candidate can sit quietly before coming into the interview?
- Do you have water available?
- Can you offer alternatives or adaptations to tasks e.g. longer time to present; different format; opportunity for a work trial?
- Where practicable, consult with any applicants who have indicated that they may need adjustments.
- If someone may require additional time e.g. to process information or need longer to respond, it may be better to schedule their appointment at the end of the interview session so that others are not kept waiting.

- Consider undertaking video interviews as an alternative format to interviewing face to face.
- Does the chair the applicant is sitting in support someone with problems with tone e.g. co-ordination difficulties and so they may appear to slump, or for someone with a stammer who may need an upright chair to manage their breathing techniques?
- Someone with a communication disorder may use Text-to-Speech software in an interview and so may require a table and desk to use this and the ability to project the answers as well as speakers for the panel to hear the responses.

For the applicant

- Give clear information about what will be expected at the interview.
- Give a list of what needs to be brought along to the interview and email/post this information to the candidate.
- Send clear instructions on how to get to the interview. Using a postcode and a map helps, along with transport options where possible.
- Tell the applicant how much time the interview will take and what is to be expected during the interview.
- Describe any tasks that will be asked of the candidate and give some indication of the content/type of question that may be asked.
- Give information about the interview panel e.g. numbers and who will be there and their roles.

- Consider how the tasks asked in the interview reflect what is expected of the individual in reality in the job, regarding level of skill and the time allowed. Reflect if the job itself has on-site training and time to gain the skills: how job ready does the individual need to be?
- Consider a work trial as an alternative to an interview.
- If an individual has disclosed, then discuss the need for Access to Work support at this stage.

Interview stage

- Introduce all the people on the interview panel by name and have name badges or cards where possible.
- Be aware that direct eye contact may vary and be difficult for some candidates, and may make them feel uncomfortable. However, this does not mean they are not interested or not listening.
- Consider how 'sociable' someone needs to be for the particular job being interviewed and don't judge this aspect if it not an essential skill.
- If there are standard group tasks, could this be done one to one or adjusted for the candidate?
- Ask questions based on the candidate's real life/past experiences.
- Ask one question at a time rather than multi-part questions.
- Be patient and allow extra time for answering questions.

- Don't fill in responses if the individual is slow to respond, allow time.
- Avoid ambiguous questions. If answers are brief then prompt with further questions to seek more information.
- Be prepared to repeat questions (slowly) if the candidate seems uncertain, or re-present the information.
- Be aware that questions may be interpreted literally, e.g. 'How did you get to where you are now?' . . . 'On the bus'.
- Ignore 'fillers', such as 'you know', as this may be a mechanism for the individual to process information.
- If specific tasks are being tested then ask if additional time has been requested. Consider the setting where this takes place such as in a quiet room, especially if novel tasks are being asked of the candidate.
- If you are paying expenses to get to the interview, do not ask the individual to fill in a form, especially if this is handwritten.
- If oral responses are difficult e.g. a stammer, then offering the interviewee the chance to respond in a written format or using IT there and then may be an option.
  http://www.stammeringlaw.org.uk/ employment/ra.htm

Disclosure

- An employee may choose to disclose their difficulties to you as their employer. It is also within their rights not to disclose their disability. It has to be recognised that such a disclosure may have caused the employee a lot of anxiety and an understanding of this is important.
- As an employer, you have a responsibility to make reasonable adjustments if a disabled employee feels that they are at a disadvantage in the workplace in relation to an employee without a disability and have disclosed to you their disability. If they have not disclosed, it is harder for you to do anything specific for them.
- The employee or potential employee can disclose on an application form, before an interview (if they want some adjustments to be made at the time), in the interview, or once in the job.
- If the individual discloses, then you can:

  - make reasonable adjustments to allow them to carry on doing their work or to be on an equal footing during their recruitment process and throughout their employment.
  - apply to Access to Work – a government programme to help people with disabilities into work. They can help fund adjustments and also supply training for your workplace.

  - offer them a guaranteed interview if you are part of the two tick system *http://www.pluss.org.uk/2-ticks-positive-about-disability-symbol*

Starting the job

- Pre-visit orientation for the job may reduce anxiety and allow the individual to understand the set-up of the organisation and layout of the building, including where toilets and the canteen are, as well as work areas.
- Any information on the organisation should be sent out before the start of the job with clear expectations of the day and breaks, holiday provision, map of where the workplace setting is etc.
- It is useful to provide written information that can be emailed to the individual, as well as oral information, so that they can read this (or someone else can read it with them) at another time.
- Go through the job description in detail at a quiet time and describe what is expected of the individual on a day-to-day basis specifically, and how and when these expectations will be measured.
- Be specific about hours, dress code (especially if dress code changes on some days), and social expectations including lunch and coffee breaks. Do people usually go alone for lunch? Is there a 'kitty' for tea and coffee?

- Discuss any rules about the workplace e.g. no alcohol on site, no smoking, no swearing, how to report illness etc.
- Explain the hierarchy in the organisation. Give a visual map as well to support this where possible.
- If there are issues of confidentiality explain these to the individual explicitly.
- Give a written list of terms and phrases that may be used in the workplace such as the use of acronyms. The individual could also make a photo list with a smartphone if there are specific items such as technical equipment or signs they need to identify so they can search for them, and also learn specific spellings.
- Allocate a mentor to assist a new employee, where appropriate, until they are settled in.
- Consider a mentor if the workplace changes in layout or in the type of work the employee is being asked to complete.
- If there are processes to be learnt, plan for someone to show the individual how to do these. Videoing the tasks required may also help the individual to replay this if required e.g. on their smartphone. Encourage the individual to make notes/audio reminders as they go so they can recall later.
- Check what organisational techniques the individual uses already, such as a diary system, to ensure this links with the job processes and how others can interlink with these e.g. pass on information; ask for work to be completed.

- Discuss with the individual what reasonable adjustments may be appropriate and how these can be best achieved. Ask them what or who has helped them in the past and where difficulties have arisen.
- Discuss how Access to Work assessments could be arranged with them to check out what adjustments could be put in place.
- Consider ways for individuals to disclose their difficulties to others and how this should be appropriately relayed to the line manager and peers.
- Discuss skills gaps that may require additional training e.g. answering phones, data entry, meeting others, working as a team, specific task, asking for help when uncertain, time management issues, organisational issues.
- Is any training that is undertaken being delivered using a multi-sensory approach i.e. talk, shown, limiting words or having pictures to assist, so that someone with Dyslexia/ Dyspraxia/Autism/Communication Impairment is not put at a disadvantage? Are there notes available that can be annotated?

Day to day in the job – making reasonable adjustments

- When making reasonable adjustments, they need to be considered in the context of what is practical and reasonable. This may be adaptation of a task, provision of equipment, and support. Some adjustments are about attitude and willingness to seek alternative ways of doing a job and should be considered as part of 'business as usual'.

- Below are some examples of documents relating to this:

  - *http://www.equalityhumanrights.com/ advice-and-guidance/before-the-equality- act/guidance-for-employers-pre-october-10/ areas-of-responsibility/making-reasonable- adjustments-for-disabled-employees/*
  - *https://www.gov.uk/reasonable-adjustments- for-disabled-workers*
  - *http://www.re-adjust.co.uk/5799/dyslexia-in- the-workplace*
  - *http://www.equalityni.org/archive/pdf/ Employingpeoplewithautism.pdf*

- See Chapter 2 **for reasonable adjustments for specific conditions**
- See Chapter 13 **for reasonable adjustments for specific settings**

Some examples of reasonable adjustments

- Consider the workplace setting. A workspace area that is away from general office traffic and reduced visual distractions such as clutter may be beneficial to the employee.
- Some individuals may have specific needs because of their difficulties, such as having a consistent base to work from, a quiet area, or

the ability to cut out noise (e.g. by wearing headphones), or a regular place to put their personal possessions.

- Break down new skills/tasks into parts and demonstrate as well as telling the person how to do them. Allow sufficient practice time to master a new skill.
- Be patient – it may take a little longer, but once the individual has the skills in place they will be invaluable.
- Define clear plans and time outcomes expected of the individual. Check for understanding. If these time plans are not being achieved, sit down together and discuss why this is so, and what else can be put in place to support the individual.
- Avoid ambiguous instructions such as 'You could do this' . . . 'Please do this' is better.
- Provide regular meetings for review and the opportunity to seek clarification – these don't need to be long.
- Provide regular feedback to the individual and be specific on what is good work or where the individual needs assistance. Demonstrate what you expect and not just say it, where possible.
- Consider how tasks can be broken into parts through the day in order to remember all the parts of the job (including tasks that they are both good and not so good at).
- Be prepared to set up report templates for repeated work if in an office setting.
- Use of technology can assist some individuals

such as Speech-to-Text software, Text-to-Speech software, spell checkers, change in font, screen magnifiers depending on the job (see Chapter 8 for more information on appropriate software).

- Avoid asking an individual to read information aloud, present in front of peers, write on a white board, or take minutes in a meeting without prior agreement.
- Discuss how the individual should address colleagues, line managers and customers/clients in differing formats of communication:

  ○ Speaking to line managers – what is the rule e.g. first name, Mr xx?
  ○ Emailing and texting – how should they start the email (what salutation e.g. Hiya,or Dear Sir, or Hi) and end the communication with a colleague or a potential customer (e.g. best wishes, kind regards) (an x kiss at the end is not usually appropriate to someone who is not closest to you!).
  ○ Create a template if necessary for letters, emails, and reports.
  ○ Greeting form – which terms are unacceptable e.g. darling, dear, babe, hun for someone you are not close to. Be explicit.

- Be clear about processes if the individual is sick. If they have communication difficulties adjust the process so they don't need to phone in.
- See Chapter 6 for more detail on this.

Job Carving

Job carving is a term for customising job duties and can used in different circumstances: it can be used to create specialised job roles or to create a job using the best skills the individual has. It has been used in supported employment with individuals with an intellectual disability, but can be a good way of considering ways of optimising the work performance in any area of employment by matching the jobs to the skills of the people rather than squeezing people into the job descriptions e.g. someone who is careful and meticulous could do the ordering of stationary and other goods across a business. However, it does need to be seen as being fair to other employees:

*http://www.griffinhammis.com/publications/
    carving.pdf*

Managing times of change

There are several situations which may create anxiety or difficulties for someone with a Specific Learning Difficulty and when reasonable adjustments may need to be reconsidered.

This may be in the following situations:

- Following a transfer or re-alignment of responsibilities
- To access a training event/course
- To participate in a career development scheme

- Following a promotion or new role
- Following an intense period of rehabilitation or treatment
- Attending a meeting, seminar or conference, and travelling away
- Due to implementation of new working methods or technology e.g. introduction of new computer systems
- Following a period of absence
- During a grievance or disciplinary procedure
- Due to a change in personal circumstances.

Each one may present different challenges. However, the principles remain the same. It is also important to remember the emotional overlay that change can cause and that feelings of anxiety on top of a baseline of having a challenge may cause a tipping point.

Changing jobs, changing roles
Some employees will excel at their jobs and will move forward in their chosen employment. They will go far and be successfully promoted and this may trigger changing roles and responsibilities. Always consider going through the processes of the 'new job' and being clear what is to be expected and whether new or differing reasonable adjustments will be required. A new position may require new skills to be learnt and specific training required e.g. someone may now be doing presentations, or going out to meetings having before been in a non-customer facing position.

Another example is where someone may now need to complete reports or expense sheets but did not need to in a previous role.

Changing line managers
Any change for some individuals, especially those who may be on the autism spectrum may cause great anxiety. Knowing the ways and manner of one manager may have taken some time to work out for the individual, and vice versa, for the manager to understand the best ways to work with that individual.

Preparing both manager and individual for any change is important to ensure a smooth transition. The line manager may need to know the best ways of communicating information e.g. by sending emails rather than giving a series of oral instructions. They may need to understand what reasonable adjustments have already been put in place and they may also require staff training.

Return to work

Consider six stages to plan for a return to work.

Gain an understanding of the employee's abilities and needs
Ask the employee what limitations they have. Plan a meeting with them by phone, on the web (e.g. through Skype) or face to face. If they have had a specific illness either physical or psychological, have they been 'signed off' as medically fit?

Do they need a graduated return to work over a period of time because of lack of fitness or increased anxiety?

Before the employee returns, brief the employee on what's been happening in work, such as any changes in policy or practice. Remember also to keep them informed of day-to-day life in the business so they don't feel they have missed out a lot during their absence.

Review the job description and job requirements

Has anything changed since they were last in post?

Can they do the core elements of the job still? e.g. if they work in a noisy environment and coped but find this much harder now, what changes need to be made (where possible) to allow them to do their job?

Implement workplace modifications or adjustments

First talk with the employee and see what adjustments need to be made e.g. time to go to a medical appointment or flexible working hours? Do they need an Access to Work assessment to discuss further reasonable adjustment changes?

An agreed Return to Work Plan

A Return to Work Plan is a helpful document that you (or an assisting rehabilitation professional) should prepare for any return to work. The Return to Work Plan needs to clearly include:

- The employee's job title
- A summary of duties
- Starting and finishing times
- Break times
- Any specific restrictions or recommendations (as per medical certificate)
- The details of the supervisors or managers responsible for monitoring progress of the Return to Work Plan
- A time schedule for review, if a gradual return to work is in place.

The Return to Work Plan should be gone through in detail with all significant parties on the day the employee returns to work. All parties should, once they have agreed, sign the Return to Work Plan.

Regular review is important to ensure that progress is made and adequate support given.

Working with co-workers
Discuss with the employee if they want their condition or medical status to be discussed with others and gain consent. Having co-workers on board to understand the challenges can help considerably, with them assisting and coming up with ideas on how to make some adjustments.

As a manager be aware of potential concerns from co-workers and deal with these promptly.

Consider the need for providing awareness training as co-workers may have varying experience of meeting or working with people with conditions such as ADHD or Autism Spectrum Disorders.

Phased return to work

Almost no-one is ever fully fit when they return to work after an illness (physical or mental) and it takes some time to recover speed, strength and agility of both mind and body. Waiting for people to be become 100 per cent fit for their work before allowing them back is therefore unrealistic – it lengthens absences unnecessarily and may ultimately even compromise their future employability.

It is common sense to adjust work in the early days after an extended spell of absence to promote full recovery and to ease the individual back into productive employment.

Discuss what reasonable adjustments need to be made. A change in health status may require some additional adjustments short term e.g. if someone has been ill with depression and Autism Spectrum Disorder.

To start with they may require:

- Flexible working hours
- Avoidance of coming to work at peak rush hour times
- Quiet area to work in
- Time to see a specialist or attend counselling sessions
- Reduced volume of work to regain confidence
- Regular reviews to monitor progress and phased increase in workload.

Link to guidance for managing employees' return to work following long-term sickness absence:

http://www.bohrf.org.uk/downloads/
    Managing_Rehabilitation-Guidance.pdf

CHAPTER 14

Making reasonable adjustments for specific workplace settings

Office setting

Environment

- Look at the current workspace – is there a need to be placed in a different position or more space e.g. away from the 'flow of traffic'?
- Is there a need for a quiet space or quiet place to be able to go to at break times away from others?
- Discuss if there are any triggers – what makes symptoms worse e.g. sound, lighting, work position? For some people noise such as people or machinery can cause high levels of stress and irritability. Can the individual be placed away from the flow of 'traffic' i.e. people passing by?
- Is the view of lots of people in an open plan office distracting? Could the individual sit in a booth, cubicle or with dividers, or face a wall?

- Check that spaces between desks are reasonable to allow someone to pass through without knocking themselves if they have poor spatial awareness.
- 'Hot-desking' (moving around from desk to desk) rather than having their own desk may be hard to do for some peoplewhere self-organisation is a challenge. Having one place to keep possessions and a constant place to work from can be good for individuals with ASD and other hidden impairments.

Dealing with noise or movement distractions in the workplace

Some level of distraction in the workplace is unavoidable. These tips may help minimise the level of distraction experienced in the workplace:

- If the desk is in a busy area a discussion with the employee and line manager to see if a quieter part of the office would be a better place. If the individual is on the main thoroughfare where there is a lot of 'traffic' i.e. other people passing, could s/he be moved away from the flow and facing into a corner for example, so less distracted by movement as well.
- Consider discussing the use of earplugs or listening to some music. Check that this does not have health and safety implications or affect the ability to do the job or impact on others e.g. answering the phone, hearing colleagues asking for some information.

- Co-workers may interrupt work flow from time to time to make 'small talk'. This is about topics other than work. If giving guidance to an employee suggest that it is polite to have a brief chat, for a few minutes, but if the conversation is continuing after that then it fine to excuse themselves from the conversation.
- Below are some suggestions for polite ways to leave a chat to get back to work. Don't forget to smile and use a friendly tone of voice:

  ○ 'I've got a lot of work on right now; can we chat about this over lunch?'
  ○ 'Let's talk about this after; I need to finish this piece of work off'.

- Interruptions can affect some individual's concentration greatly. The use of 'do not disturb' signs can make it easier to tell someone non-verbally not to interrupt work flow.
- Encourage the individual to finish off what they are working on e.g. make a note, so they know where to resume.

At the desk, working at the computer

- Supply anti-glare screen filter if required.
- Discuss the need for breaks, even standing up to stretch every hour.
- Discuss means of alternating computer work with other tasks where possible, especially where the individual has a short attention span or tires easily.

- Consider seating, especially where someone has poor posture e.g. with DCD/Dyspraxia.
- Discuss the need for a specialist mouse, keyboard, and footrest to ensure a good ergonomic position.
- Discuss the need for specific software e.g. TTS,STT, changing the colour of the background screen, use of specific fonts.
- If the individual has Dyslexia, discuss whether printing reports on beige or buff paper is of assistance.
- Using a photocopier may be difficult for some where there is a need to follow a process in a sequence. Break the task into parts and demonstrate it, and allow practice.
- Use colour coding for box files and folders and clearly label them so that reports and papers can be easily found.
- Encourage and demonstrate how to keep the work area tidy if there are organisational difficulties.
- Give adequate time for the individual to read through documents/information before a meeting. Provide an executive summary of key important points.
- When sending documents or instructions to someone:

  - highlight salient points
  - set up templates where possible to reduce text entry (and spelling errors)

- use plain English, be concise and check the readability of documents and instructions.

- Discuss, if necessary, with co-workers that some people do not like their belongings moved and this may cause upset e.g. those with obsessional traits.
- Mark trays for post and papers so they can be sorted quickly.
- A good position at the desk includes:

  - arms relaxed by the individual's side
  - screen should be set approximately an arm's length from the individual
  - top of the screen about eye level
  - forearms should be parallel with the desk
  - feet flat on the floor or on a foot rest.

  http://www.nhs.uk/livewell/workplacehealth/ pages/howtositcorrectly.aspx

Meetings

- Having to respond when nervous may be harder to do in a group setting, especially if someone has a processing or communication impairment. Discuss what is the preferred method of introducing themselves e.g. going first.
- Use of name badges can assist with introductions but may disadvantage someone with a visual impairment.
- Avoid asking someone with Dyslexia/Dyspraxia to stand up and be the note taker without prior discussion.

- If someone has writing difficulties, then avoid asking them to be a note taker.
- Use of a digital recorder to take notes of a meeting can help in order to access afterwards in case information has been missed.
- Use of a tablet with a spell checker built in may be easier to take notes than pen and paper.
- Taking photos of documents/spreadsheets, or from a flip chart using a phone or tablet may be helpful to review later.

Communication methods between team members

- Agree means of communication e.g. give verbal as well as written instructions or using voice mail as opposed to written memos.
- Highlighting important aspects of emails may alert someone with ADHD to the areas they need to address first and prioritise.
- Avoid metaphors or jokes in written communication which could be misinterpreted.
- Avoid giving multiple instructions.
- Be aware there may be difficulties listening to the information in a noisy setting.
- Write down important information, as well saying it.
- Encourage the individual to take notes in the manner that best suits them.
- Follow up meetings with an action plan.
- When presenting information do so using both words and, where appropriate, diagrams.

- Give clear concise and direct instructions; do not hint or make assumptions that you have been understood. Check understanding.
- Be direct and face the person when you are talking to them. Someone with ASD may not be aware that what you are saying to the group is being addressed to them as well.

People facing/sales/retail

- Good organisation is essential in a sales job. If the individual is going out to meet people, then organising their diary is important and using reminders built into the phone including the appointment time, place (including post code) and any specific details of the customer.
- Retail work may include folding clothes and this may be harder for someone with DCD/Dyspraxia. Consider moving them to a task that does not require this. Someone with ASD who has good attention to detail may be ideally placed in arranging items to order and in sequence and in a set manner.
- If the job is customer facing, it may be helpful to prepare scripts to go through with the individual if they have social and communication difficulties e.g. how to greet customers and avoiding asking personal information.
- Discuss any health and safety issues explicitly with the individual.

- If the individual has to work out bills etc. and
they have difficulties with numbers, encourage
them to call out the numbers while using the
calculator and checking them with the
customer. A talking calculator may be helpful.

Catering

There are many different jobs in catering with
different challenges:

- Someone with fine motor skills difficulties (e.g.
Dyspraxia/DCD) may find chopping and
preparing food harder to do. Ensuring the
person is stable while doing these tasks is
important. Rubber handled tools, where
appropriate, can be helpful.
- A waiter or waitress may need to remember a
series of instructions. This may be harder to
write down if handwriting is poor. Some
restaurants now use digital tablets which
minimises the need to write.
- Appropriate shoes with nonslip soles can help
someone with balance difficulties.
- Using a one handled tray may be easier for
some individuals with co-ordination difficulties.
- Tray carrying carts could be used instead.

Call Centre

There are a number of different jobs in a call centre
that may be great for someone with a Specific
Learning Difficulty as they can follow a set routine,

or be very hard as they require speed, accuracy and the ability to work under time pressure. There is a big difference between an outgoing call centre job, where the caller makes the call and has to initiate the conversation, and the inbound call job, where the individual may be responding to a set of queries for example. The latter may be easier for someone with a communication difficulty as the responses may be more scripted.

- A job with a script and very standardised procedures may be easier for someone who does not deal with change well. Cold calling may be very difficult for someone with language and communication difficulties, where listening and responding skills need to be excellent to be able to quickly engage with the caller at the other end of the phone.
- Encourage the individual to practise the scripts and to have them in front of them as a prompt.
- If outgoing calls need to be made, preparing some notes beforehand can assist someone if their memory is poor, or if they are very nervous. This can be discussed with the line manager or a mentor.
- A modified script may need to be considered if an individual has difficulties with articulating (saying) specific words.
- If accuracy is important e.g. for recording addresses and numbers, this may be harder for someone with Dyslexia, or Dyscalculia.

Templates for recording may assist. Minimising free text entry may be of assistance where possible.

- Working at speed and accuracy may be harder for someone with DCD/Dyspraxia, and they may need additional time to learn the tasks if there are multiple components.

Science, technology, nursing, dental, caring, medical, allied health professionals

Specialist jobs usually require a specialist assessment to unpack the job description and see where the barriers are and reasonable adjustments need to be made. There is usually also a need to satisfy the professional body that the individual is 'fit to practise'.

- Consider the environment the individual is being placed in and whether this changes or is consistent e.g. a student on work placement may need to be placed in several different work settings requiring different adjustments. This may highlight new challenges such as planning travel, meeting new people, or learning new skills.
- Consider the specific tasks that are expected of the job and whether adaptations can be made or not e.g. taking blood; putting up a drip; emptying a catheter bag, and if someone has very poor fine motor co-ordination whether adjustments will be adequate or not.

- Break down the task and consider where the challenge lies.
- Are there abbreviations that need to be made clear. Encourage the individual to keep a log of these on their phone or in a notebook.
- Create a log of specific spellings for medication. Have a checking system in place for administration of drugs if reading or recording is difficult. Drugs with similar names should be highlighted.
- Go through specific forms and processes that need to be completed and give time to familiarise the processes.
- Have some 'sample' or 'model' reports for different types of documentation, particularly to show the level and content expected.
- If recording notes is difficult to do, then allow the individual to use STT (Speech-to-Text software) and then sign it as their work.

There are some useful documents that may give some additional specific guidance:

http://www.nmc-uk.org/students/good-health-and-good-character-for-students-nurses-and-midwives/reasonable-adjustments/
http://bma.org.uk/practical-support-at-work/doctors-well-being/reasonable-adjustments
http://www.heacademy.ac.uk/assets/ps/documents/practice_guides/practice_guides/supporting_students_aspergers_syndrome_rpg.pdf

Dyslexia, Dyspraxia and Dyscalculia: a toolkit for nursing staff

http://www.rcn.org.uk/__data/assets/pdf_file/
0003/333534/003835.pdf

CHAPTER 15

Useful organisations

Disability and the law

The Disability Rights Commission (DRC)

www.drc-gb.org

Government information

www.direct.gov.uk/en/employment/index.htm
https://www.gov.uk/discrimination-your-
    rights/types-of-discrimination
https://www.gov.uk/rights-disabled-
    person/employment

Equality and Human Rights Commission

http://www.equalityhumanrights.com/advice-and-
    guidance/new-equality-act-guidance/
    equality-act-starter-kit/
http://odi.dwp.gov.uk/docs/wor/new/ea-guide.pdf
http://www.acas.org.uk/chttphandler.ashx?id=
    2833&p=0

Government Disability Programmes

UK

Disability Confident Campaign

This is a link to a range of useful materials to assist employers including case studies and posters that can be downloaded, launched in 2013:

> *https://www.gov.uk/government/publications/*
>   *the-disability-confident-campaign*
> *https://www.gov.uk/government/publications/*
>   *employing-disabled-people-and-people-with-*
>   *health-conditions/employing-disabled-people-*
>   *and-people-with-health-conditions*

Access to Work

This is a UK government funded scheme to provide support and guidance from before employment e.g. at the interview stage, and within employment. The following is a guide to the programme:

> *http://www.dwp.gov.uk/docs/employer-guide-*
>   *atw.pdf*

Hidden Impairment Toolkit

This is a website with resources for employers on how to assist individuals with hidden impairments:

> *http://www.hing.org.uk/*

Additional detailed information to download freely is also on:

http://www.doitprofiler.com/resources.aspx

Australia

*https://www.gov.uk/government/publications/
the-disability-confident-campaign*

Contact details of organisations associated with specific conditions

ADHD

ADDISS
ADDISS is The National Attention Deficit Disorder Information and Support Service. They provide people-friendly information and resources about Attention Deficit Hyperactivity Disorder to anyone who needs assistance – parents, sufferers, teachers or health professionals.

http://www.addiss.co.uk/

AADD-UK
The main aims of AADD-UK are raising awareness of ADHD in adulthood, advancing the education of professionals and the public at a national and local level in the UK to ensure that all adults with ADHD regardless of age, health, ethnicity, socio-economic status, and religion have fair and equitable access

to health, social, employment, and other services as needed, and to promote and support research in the field of adult ADHD.

http://aadduk.org/

Anxiety

http://www.anxietyuk.org.uk/
http://www.social-anxiety.org.uk/

Autism/Asperger's Syndrome

The National Autistic Society
This organisation provides information, support and pioneering services. The website has plenty of information for individuals going to university such as:

- a list of colleges for individuals with autism or Asperger's Syndrome
- advice on choosing and applying for university
- starting university – including information on study skills and what to expect.

http://www.autism.org.uk/
http://www.autism.org.uk/living-with-autism/
    adults-with-autism-or-asperger-syndrome.aspx
http://www.autism.org.uk/
    about-autism/research/
    information-for-pupils-and-individuals/
    autism-information-for-he-individuals-
    studying-the-condition.aspx

Autism Northern Ireland

http://www.autismni.org/

Irish Autism Ireland

http://www.autismireland.ie/

Bipolar Disorder

Bipolaruk

http://www.bipolaruk.org.uk/

Seeme

http://www.seemescotland.org.uk/findoutmore/
aboutmentalhealthproblemsandstigma/
bipolar-disorder

Depression

Depression Alliance

The following organisation works to relieve and prevent depression:

http://www.depressionalliance.org/

Living life to the full

http://www.llttf.com/

Mind
This is for anyone with a mental health problem to have somewhere to turn for advice and support:

http://www.mind.org.uk/

Sane
This is a charity working to improve quality of life for anyone affected by mental illness:

http://www.sane.org.uk/

Moodgym
Games and activities to help with depression:

https://moodgym.anu.edu.au/welcome

Cognitive Behavioural Therapy
This has information on cognitive behavioural therapy and links to other sites:

*http://www.rcpsych.ac.uk/expertadvice/
treatments/cbt.aspx*

Dyslexia and Dyscalculia

The British Dyslexia Association:
The vision of the British Dyslexia Association is a Dyslexia-friendly society enabling all dyslexic people to reach their potential.

Below is a list of some of the online information resources that they provide for individuals:

- information for Higher Education individuals
- screening and assessment information
- books on Dyslexia

http://www.bdadyslexia.org.uk/
http://www.bdadyslexia.org.uk/about-
   dyslexia/schools-colleges-and-universities/
   dyscalculia.html

Dyslexia Action

http://dyslexiaaction.org.uk/

The Dyslexia Association Ireland

The Dyslexia Association Ireland provides a free information service to the public. Services offered include: psycho-educational assessment of children and adults, group and individual specialised tuition, teachers' courses, summer schools, speakers for schools and parent groups.

http://www.dyslexia.ie/

Dyslexia Scotland

http://www.dyslexiascotland.org.uk/
http://www.dyslexiascotland.org.uk/adults

Dyspraxia/Developmental Co-ordination Disorder

Dyspraxia Foundation:
The Dyspraxia Foundation supports individuals and families affected by Dyspraxia.
Online resources available from the Dyspraxia Foundation website include:

- advice for adults
- living with Dyspraxia and useful contacts
- daily life – coping strategies

http://www.dyspraxiafoundation.org.uk/

Also see www.movementmattersuk.org for more information.

Dyspraxia Association Ireland

http://www.dyspraxia.ie/

Obsessive Compulsive Disorder

OCD-UK
This site offers information for patients and carers on the condition as well as a location finder service for support groups:

http://www.ocduk.org/

Speech, Language and Communication Impairments

AFASIC

Afasic is a UK charity that helps children, young people, and adults and their families with hidden disability of speech, language and communication impairments. They have a number of free leaflets available and a comprehensive website.

http://www.afasic.org.uk/publications/
    planning-for-life-after-16/
http://www.afasic.org.uk

Tourette's Syndrome

Tourettes Action

Tourettes Action is a charity working to make life better for people with Tourette's Syndrome.

http://www.tourettes-action.org.uk/

Other helpful organisations

British Association for Supported Employment

The British Association for Supported Employment is the national trade association representing hundreds of agencies involved in securing employment for people with disabilities.

http://base-uk.org/

Business Disability Forum

Business Disability Forum is a membership organisation for employers to share expertise, advice, training and networking opportunities.They have created a Disability Standard.

http://businessdisabilityforum.org.uk/

The Centre for Accessibile Environments

The Centre for Accessible Environments (CAE) is an authority on inclusive design.

http://cae.org.uk/index.html

Disability Action Alliance

A cross sector network of organisations committed to making a difference to the lives of disabled people by designing and delivering innovative changes and identifying and spreading good practice, especially at local level.

http://disabilityactionalliance.org.uk/

Disability Rights UK

Putting disability equality and human rights into practice across society

http://disabilityrightsuk.org/

Royal College of Psychiatrists

Information and links to resources for employers who are looking to support their employees at work so that they remain productive and healthy.

http://www.rcpsych.ac.uk/usefulresources/
workandmentalhealth/employer.aspx

Additional links to other organisations for managers

https://whitehall-admin.production.
alphagov.co.uk/government/uploads/system/
uploads/attachment_data/file/207725/
health-and-work-resources.pdf

Blogs

Big Dog

This contains jobs and apprentice listings, articles, and information about training courses.

Details: *www.bigdog.co.uk*

NotGoingToUni

Information if you are not going to university

Details: *www.notgoingtouni.co.uk*

Plotr

Careers site for 11-24 years

Details: *www.plotr.co.uk*

National Network of Assessment Centres (NNAC)

NNAC is a UK-wide network of specialist services that work together to facilitate access to education, training, employment and personal development for disabled people. It may be particularly useful for individuals in Higher Education as they are often referred to an Assessment Centre for a DSA-funded Study Aids and Strategies Assessment.

Details: *http://www.nnac.org/*

National Careers Service

A one-stop shop for career advice. It offers tools including a CV builder, a learner record and skills health-check, as well as profiles of more than 750 jobs and information.

Details: *www.nationalcareersservice.direct.gov.uk*

List of useful books

Conflict resolution in the workplace

- Resolving Conflicts at Work: Ten Strategies for Everyone on the Job by Kenneth Cloke and Joan Goldsmith

  - *http://www.amazon.co.uk/ Resolving-Conflicts-Work-Strategies-Everyone/ dp/0470922249*

ADHD in the workplace

- A.D.D. on the Job: Making Your A.D.D. Work for You by Lynn Wiess

  - *http://www.amazon.co.uk/ D-D-Job-Making-Your-Work/dp/0878339175*

- Making ADD Work: On-the-job Strategies for Coping with Attention Deficit Disorder by Blythe Grossberg

  - *http://www.amazon.co.uk/gp/product/ 0399531998/ref=pd_lpo_k2_dp_sr_1?pf_rd_ p=103612307&pf_rd_s=lpo-top-stripe&pf_ rd_t=201&pf_rd_i=0878339175&pf_rd_m= A3P5ROKL5A1OLE&pf_rd_r= 0CFA74VTSRF3N3HRZWTN*

- ADD In the Workplace: Choices, Changes, and Challenges by Kathleen Nadeau

  - *http://www.amazon.co.uk/ADD-Workplace-Choices-Changes-Challenges/dp/0876308477*

Dyslexia in the Workplace

- Dyslexia in the Workplace by Diana Bartlett & Sylvia Moody

  - *http://www.amazon.co.uk/Dyslexia-Workplace-Introductory-Diana-Bartlett/dp/0470683740*

- Dyslexia and Employment: A Guide for Assessors, Trainers and Managers by Sylvia Moody

  - *http://www.amazon.co.uk/gp/product/0470694785/ref=pd_lpo_k2_dp_sr_2?pf_rd_p=103612307&pf_rd_s=lpo-top-stripe&pf_rd_t=201&pf_rd_i=0470683740&pf_rd_m=A3P5ROKL5A1OLE&pf_rd_r=02M3HQ5R618JHN6D32W4*

- Dyslexia: How to survive and succeed at work by Sylvia Moody

  - *http://www.amazon.co.uk/Dyslexia-How-survive-succeed-work/dp/009190708X/ref=pd_sim_b_2*

- Making Dyslexia Work for You by Vicki Goodwin

  - *http://www.amazon.co.uk/Making-Dyslexia-Work-Vicki-Goodwin/dp/0415597560/ref=pd_sim_b_3*

Dyspraxia in the Workplace

- Living with Dyspraxia: A Guide for Adults with Developmental Dyspraxia – revised edition by Mary Colley

  - *http://www.amazon.co.uk/Living-Dyspraxia-Guide-Adults-Developmental/dp/1843104520*

Useful websites and documentation

- *http://www.personneltoday.com/articles/01/07/2009/49865/disability-in-the-workplace-the-same-but-different.htm#.UaiJFJWv0yE*
- *http://www.amazon.co.uk/Copy-This-Turned-Dyslexia-Company/dp/0761143858*
- *http://www.rcn.org.uk/newsevents/congress/2010/monday/congress_today/moving_forward_challenging_Dyslexia,_Dyspraxia_and_Dyscalculia_in_the_workplace*

ADHD in the workplace

- *http://www.webmd.com/add-adhd/guide/adhd-in-the-workplace*

- *http://connect.additudemag.com/groups/ group/ADHD_at_Work/*
- *http://www.healthyplace.com/adhd/articles/ top-ten-adhd-traps-in-the-workplace/*
- This is a good article on types of jobs that suit individuals with ADHD.

  - *http://www.additudemag.com/adhd/ article/8656.html*

ASD in the workplace

- *http://www.sunderland4autism.com/ autism-in-the-workplace.html*
- *http://www.guardian.co.uk/society/2013/ mar/08/autism-career-ladder-workplace*
- *http://www.guardian.co.uk/money/2009/oct/ 17/employing-adults-with-autism*
- *http://www.equalityni.org/archive/pdf/ Employingpeoplewithautism.pdf*
- *http://askjan.org/media/asperger.html*
- *http://www.kennethrobersonphd.com/ autism-psychologist/adult-Asperger's/ five-secrets-to-workplace-success-for-adults- with-Asperger's*
- *http://zenemu.com/2011/04/working-with- someone-who-has-Asperger's-syndrome/*
- *http://www.forbes.com/2010/08/03/ asperger-syndrome-workplace-leadership- careers-autism.html*
- *http://www.autismberkshire.org.uk/ Files/Documents/employrepemployer.pdf*

Dyspraxia in the workplace

- *http://www.Dyspraxiafoundation.org.uk/ services/ad_employers.php*
- *http://www.danda.org.uk/pages/ neuro-diversity/Dyspraxia-in-the-workplace-for-employees.php*

Dyslexia in the workplace

- *http://www.bdaDyslexia.org.uk/about-Dyslexia/adults-and-business/applying-for-jobs-and-promotions.html*
- *http://www.bdaDyslexia.org.uk/about-Dyslexia/adults-and-business/help-in-finding-a-job-.html*
- *http://www.Dyslexia-help.org/employment-advice.asp*
- *http://www.personneltoday.com/articles/ 01/03/2005/29251/Dyslexia-in-the-workplace.htm*
- *http://www.bdaDyslexia.org.uk/about-Dyslexia/ adults-and-business/Dyslexia-in-the-workplace-summary-for-employers.html*
- *http://www.beatingDyslexia.com/Dyslexia-in-the-workplace.html*
- *http://www.re-adjust.co.uk/5799/Dyslexia-in-the-workplace*

Dyscalculia in the workplace

- *http://opportunities.co.uk/uncategorized/ public-sector/articles/how-to-adapt-the- workplace-for-employees-with-number- blindness-caused-by-Dyscalculia/*
- *http://www.lexxic.com/2/expertise/10/ Dyscalculia/*
- *http://www.re-adjust.co.uk/6032/ Dyscalculia*

Disclosure

- *http://www.psychologytoday.com/blog/ Asperger's-diary/201106/disability- discrimination-and-disclosure-being-out-in- the-workplace*
- *http://www.lboro.ac.uk/service/careers/ downloads/resources/leaflets/disclosing- Dyslexia-in-recruitment.pdf*
- *http://www.southampton.ac.uk/careers/ employability/myneeds/disclose.html*

Also available

Amanda Kirby's companion volume:

HOW TO SUCCEED IN COLLEGE AND UNIVERSITY WITH SPECIFIC LEARNING DIFFICULTIES:
A Guide for Students, Educators & Parents

9780285642430   Also available as an ebook

For any adult with specific learning difficulties going to college or university can be a challenge. These can present in the work and home setting, learning new skills, meeting new people, and coping with a new environment. From study skills to budgeting, from cooking to relationships, Amanda Kirby identifies routes to success in both education and socially. At the heart of this book is its practical approach to provide information and advice that is easy to access and to use.

Includes recommended free apps and software

Drawing on decades of practical, professional and academic experience Amanda Kirby provides solutions that are not only very accessible but also directs you to further reading and resources including apps and websites. Having this information all in one place is like a gold mine, as it has been previously scattered and very hard to find.

What are Specific Learning Difficulties?
Preparing for College and University.
Getting and Staying Organised.
Independent Living.
Study Skills.
Socialising and Feeling Good.
Preparing for the Workplace.
Useful contact organisations.

Specifically designed to be dyslexic friendly

Available in ebook and as a print edition

DYSPRAXIA:
Developmental Co-ordination Disorder

Dr Amanda Kirby

Dyspraxia is a condition that causes co-ordination problems. It is a hidden handicap, the children who suffer from it look the same as their friends but are dismissed as 'clumsy' rather than treated as children coping with a learning difficulty. Dyspraxia can often go undiagnosed until adulthood and is often mistaken for other conditions, such as autism, dyslexia or attention deficit disorder. In this practical and authoritative book Amanda Kirby asks the questions that parents would like answered, gives a comprehensive outline of what dyspraxia is and how it can affect a child and offers practical advice on how to help a child overcome this problem through-out their life from pre-school to adulthood.

"Dr Kirby's practical experiences and observations of children and adults with dyspraxia is highly accessible and readable, successfully dealing with a very complex subject."
'Dyslexia Contact'

What parents need most of all is information – information about causes, symptoms and other possible conditions, practical ways to improve your child's condition and how to help them to live independently as adults. This book will fulfil the need for relevant information for parents and teachers, medical professionals and play leaders, in a concise, readable and comprehensive way.

"The first wide-ranging and popular guide for parents and others who wrestle daily with the difficulties . . . It is both immensely practical and written from the heart."
'Daily Telegraph'

Available in ebook and as a print edition

THE GIFT OF DYSLEXIA:
Why some of the world's brightest people can't read and how they can learn

Ronald D. Davis

Like other dyslexics, Ronald Davis had unusual gifts of creativity and imagination, but couldn't function probably at school and it wasn't until he was an adult that he discovered techniques that allowed him to read easily. Written from personal experience of dyslexia, this breakthrough book offers unique insights into the learning problems and stigmas faced by those with the condition, and provides the author's own tried and tested techniques for overcoming and correcting it.

"At last! A book about dyslexic thinking by one who is dyslexic, and for fellow dyslexic people . . . I would recommend this book to any dyslexic and non-dyslexic person. It is a dyslexic friendly book."
'Dyslexic Contact'

The experience of being dyslexic is fully explained, from its early development to how it becomes gradually entrenched as a child comes to rely on non-verbal perception. Setting out practical step-by-step techniques, using visualisation and multisensory learning, Ronald Davis brings help to the 15% of children and adults who struggle with reading and writing because of dyslexia. In this revised and expanded edition of his classic work Ronald Davis brings real help to people who have dyslexia.

"Presented in a dyslexia friendly style . . . I would recommend this book, both for people with dyslexia and parents and teachers. It describes the problems so well, but even more importantly it radiates optimism and encouragement."
'Disability Now'

Available in ebook and as a print edition

THE FEAR OF MATHS:
How to overcome it: Sum Hope³

Steve Chinn

Organisations such as the CBI have drawn attention to a low level of maths skills in almost 50% of the working population in the UK. At its most severe level the problem may be described as 'dyscalculia' which can be considered to be the maths equivalent of dyslexia. Steve Chinn, an internationally respected special needs researcher, teacher and teacher trainer, advocates a new approach to teaching maths that aims to remove the 'fear of maths' and reduce maths anxiety. He links facts, procedures and ideas so that people can begin to make sense of maths rather than vainly try to recall the detailed steps of procedures they were shown, but never understood, in school.

"Steve Chinn regards maths as being based on a few concepts and ideas which all interlink . . . Useful to parents, teachers and support assistants helping pupils who struggle with maths concepts."
'Special Information Needs Press'

The Fear of Maths sets out to make everyday maths easier. It challenges many of the myths about maths, such as 'You have to know all your times table facts' and explains alternative techniques for adding, subtracting, dividing, multiplying, fractions and percentages, techniques that link, build and support each other. By teaching maths by understanding (rather than as a feat of memorising and recalling a series of facts and procedures) Steve Chinn demonstrates to the learner how much they already know and how they can begin to build on that knowledge to learn the maths they will need for the rest of their lives. He offers those intimidated by maths a way forward.

"A book packed with information . . . If you are serious about improving your maths skills . . . this is the book for you."
Parentsintouch.co.uk